FREEZE
FOR
FRIEZE

in collaboration with

The Royal College of Art's postcard project has been one of the most ingenious fund-raising devices of our times. It appeals on so many levels—to lovers of art, to lovers of mystery, to anyone who loves the thrill of the chase. The best thing is, everybody wins. This year, maybe more so.

Remo Ruffini and his company Moncler are partnering with the Royal College of Art to recreate the event with the title Freeze for Frieze. And the net has been cast wider for contributors. I know Remo is an ardent patron of the arts, so he'll be thrilled to see what artists, designers, musicians, writers and an entire random tribe of creative types have produced. That mix has certainly made this project's postcards the most eclectic and fascinating selection ever. So we thank all the contributors on behalf of the Royal College of Art and Remo Ruffini, and we wish you happy hunting.

TIM BLANKS [GUEST CURATOR]

Moncler took another step down the path of supporting the creativity of tomorrow, which has always been a cardinal point in the brand's philosophy; this time in London with Moncler Freeze for Frieze, an exhibition in collaboration with the prestigious cultural and educational institution, the Royal College of Art.

Moncler Freeze for Frieze took place from 7 to 9 October 2016 at the new Moncler flagship store at 26 Old Bond Street, with the aim to raise funds to cover two exceptionally talented and deserving students' full tuition for their 2–year MA degree program in Fashion and Textiles at the Royal College of Art.

"I'm very passionate about the world of art, especially how meaningful it is as a language, a means of communication, encompassing one's personal views and abilities. Art, in my opinion, is a pure expression of creativity able to capture a single moment and transport its entirety into the future. Creativity has always been a key word for Moncler. Working towards this common goal alongside a high profile institution like the Royal College of Art is a great honor for me", commented on the occasion, Remo Ruffini, Chairman and CEO of Moncler.

Moncler asked artists, fashion designers, friends of the brand chosen to represent different fields, cultural icons from the worlds of international pop-culture, music and design, and some of the renowned college's alumni and current students to donate a piece of their artwork to be exhibited for the first time ever outside the college's walls.

The 483 pieces, all in postcard format and signed only on the back, were freely donated by the artists and sold at a fixed price of 60 pounds each at the exhibition, curated by renowned journalist Tim Blanks, and staged at the Moncler flagship store during the boutique's opening event on 7 October. All funds raised were donated to the Royal College of Art.

"Being one of the most successful design companies in the world, Moncler has been a great source of inspiration to our Fashion students for many years. I'm pleased to point out that Moncler is offering something more than just inspiration here, at the Royal College of Art, through these generous contributions to the scholarship fund. It's thanks to this collaboration, in fact, that two exceptionally talented students will be able to obtain their MA degrees," said Paul Thompson, Royal College of Art Rector.

The postcards all have the specific personal touch of the individual participant who helped transform them into works of art. The artists' identities were only revealed after purchase, thereby putting internationally renowned artists, up-and-comers and new young talents on the same level playing field.

As guest-curator of Moncler Freeze for Frieze, Tim Blanks commented, 'The RCA postcard project has always been a thing of wonder to me. It's such a fabulous metaphor for the randomness of life – you could get a Hockney or you could get a hackney. So I'm very happy – and flattered to be involved in this edition. It's like a wonderful game. How good is your eye? Spot the future classic. Be surprised.'

Just as art can represent life and artists can immortalize moments in their creations, perennially giving the gift of those moments, those emotions to future generations, so too through Freeze for Frieze, Moncler affirmed its desire to "freeze" the moments depicted on the postcards, thereby making them immortal.

Moncler Freeze for Frieze has been a unique project, a kind of game of expression and imagination, but also a sign of Moncler's constant commitment to welcoming the future with generosity and good faith.

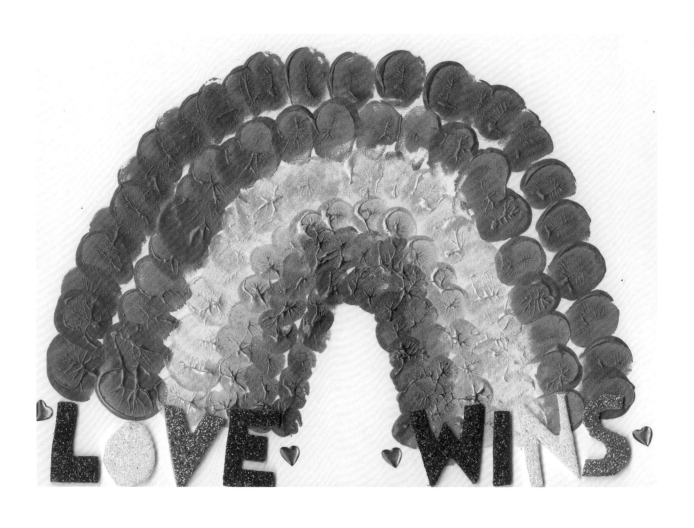

TATA SURGULADZE [FASHION DESIGNER]

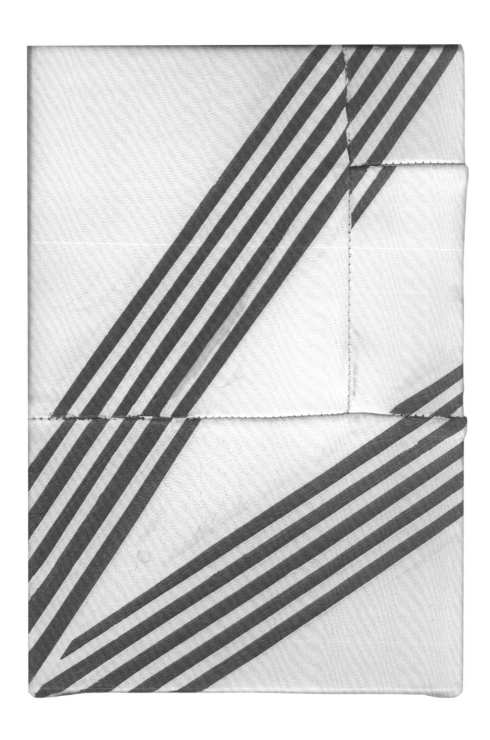

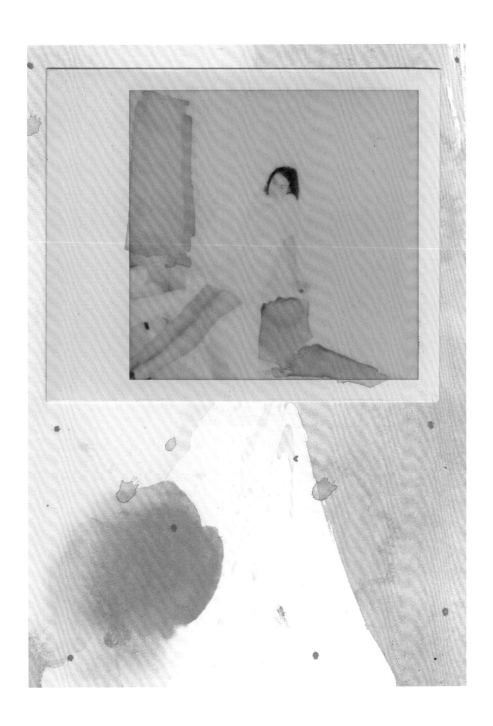

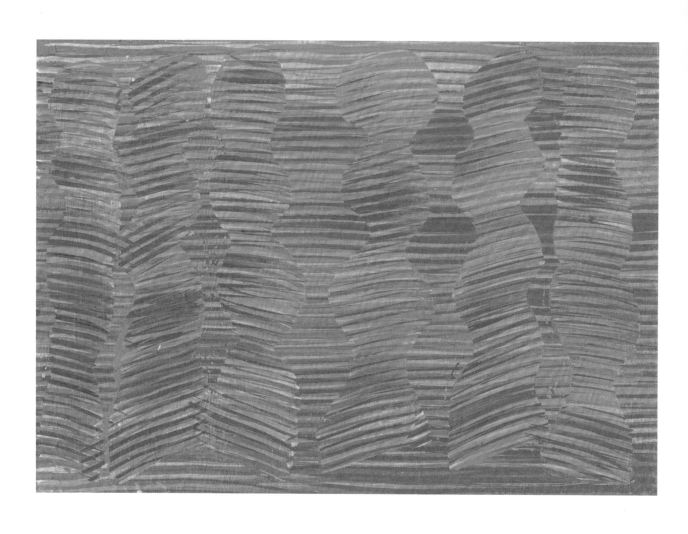

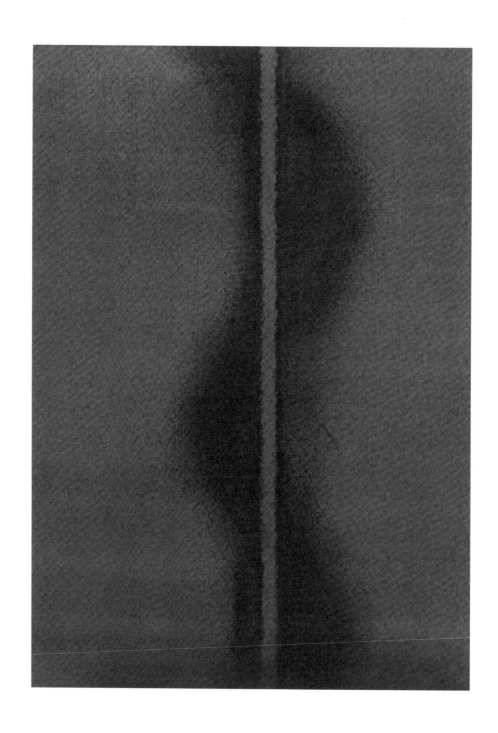

13   JOAN HECKTERMANN [ART DIRECTOR AT THE WORLD OF INTERIORS]

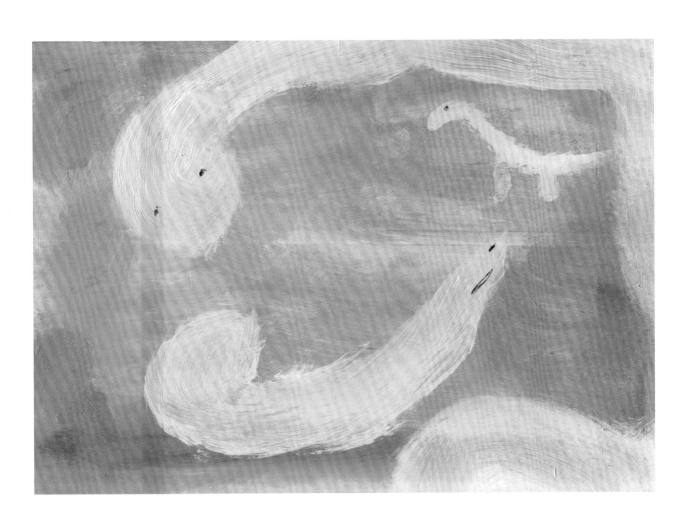

SIMON RAWLINGS [DAVID COLLINS DESIGN STUDIO]

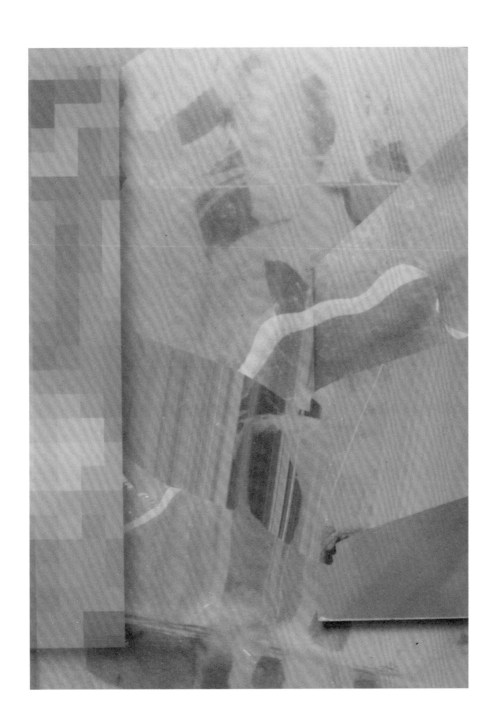

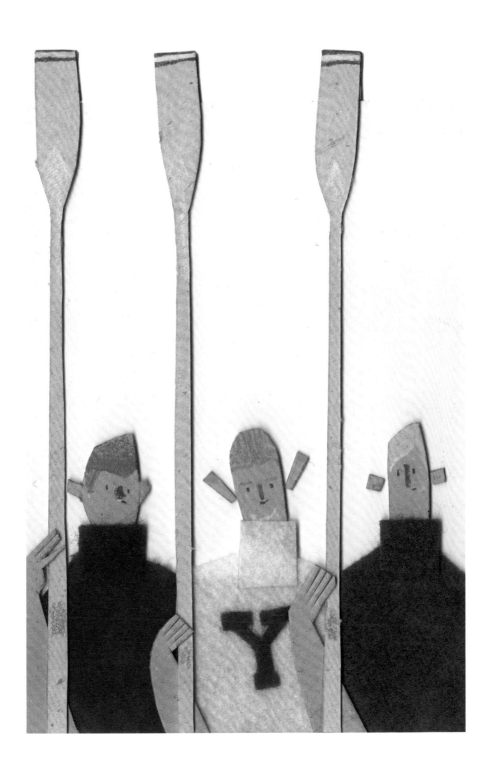

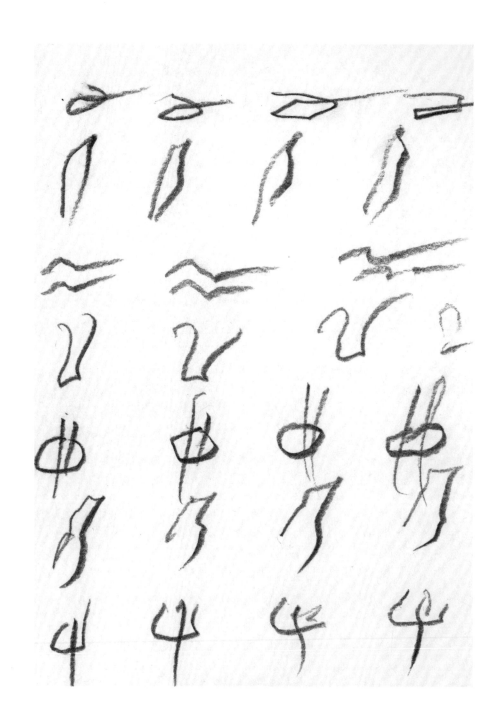

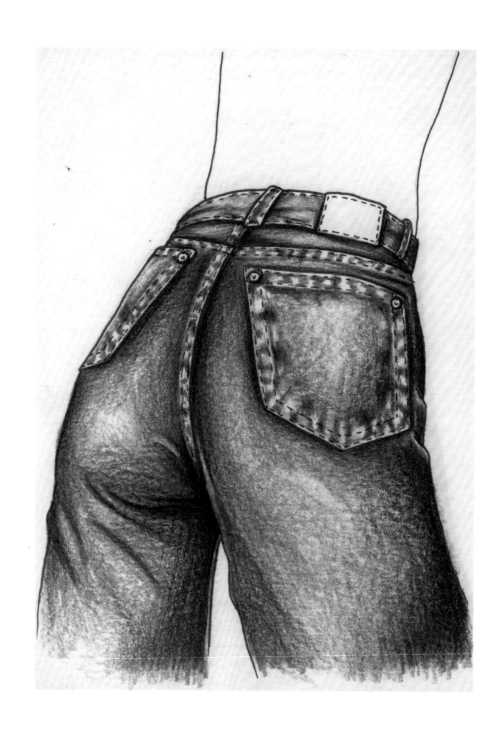

AMANDA HARLECH [CREATIVE CONSULTANT]

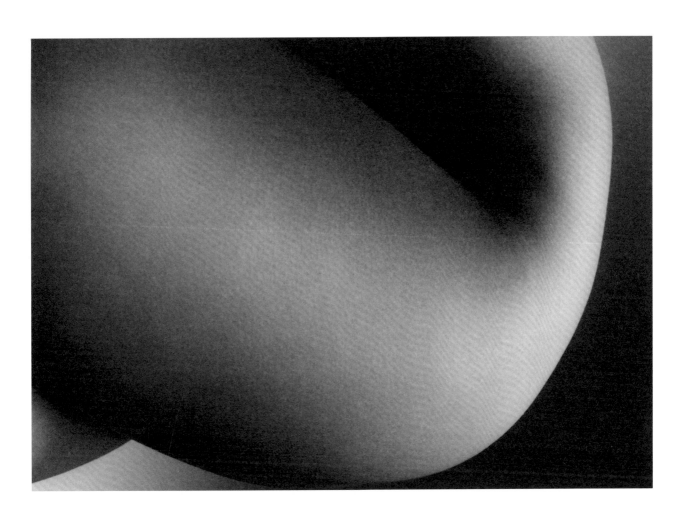

SIMON EMMETT [PHOTOGRAPHER]

NECKERCHIEF

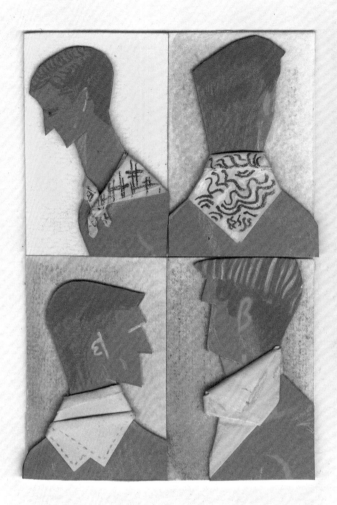

FOUR WAYS

-128-

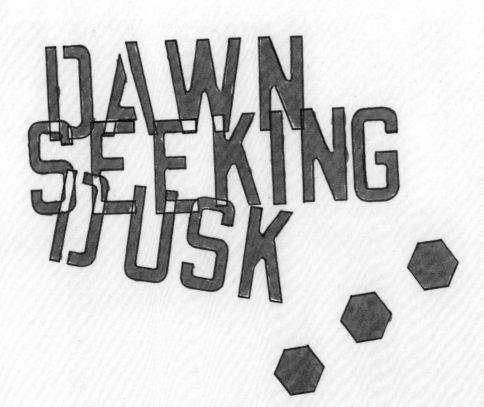

TAKE YOUR PIC(K)

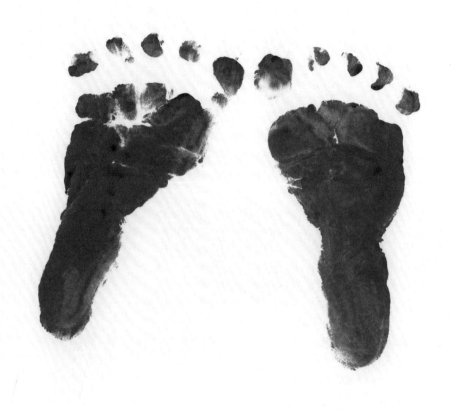

un pantalone
per tutta la
vita

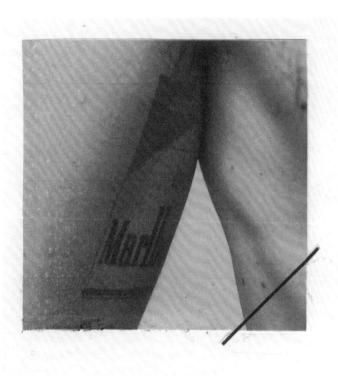

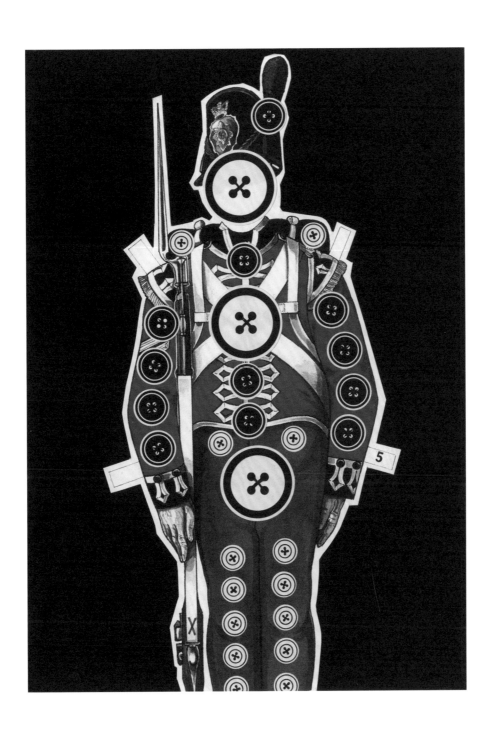

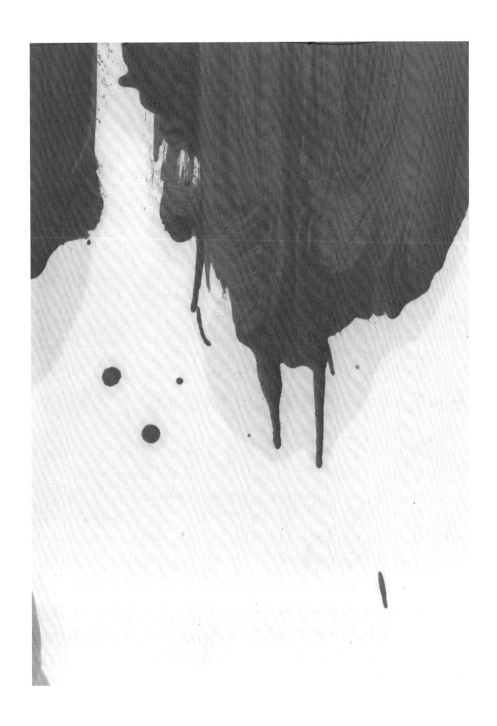

CHRISTOPHER LE BRUN [ARTIST AND PRESIDENT OF THE ROYAL ACADEMY OF ARTS]

80   CHRISTOPHER LE BRUN [ARTIST AND PRESIDENT OF THE ROYAL ACADEMY OF ARTS]

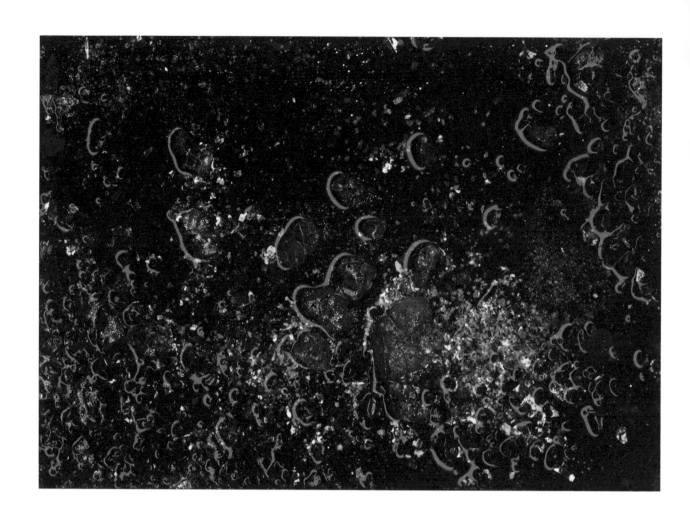

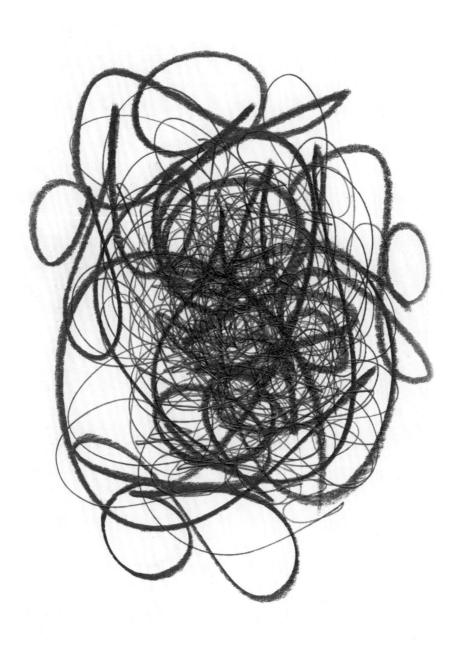

NORFOLK 16

BIG UGLY .

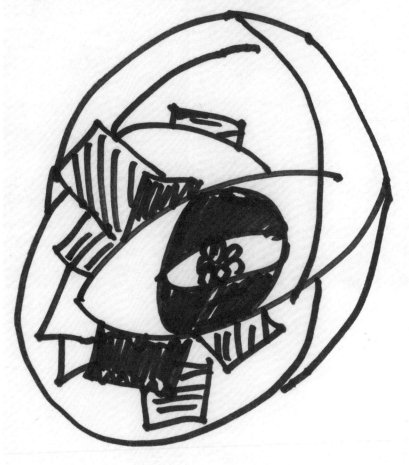

EMMA GREENHILL [PRINT DESIGNER]

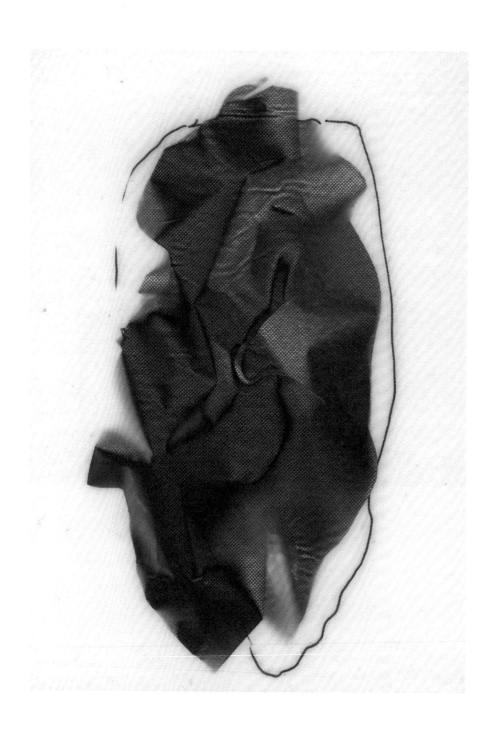

THIS IS NOT A POSTCARD

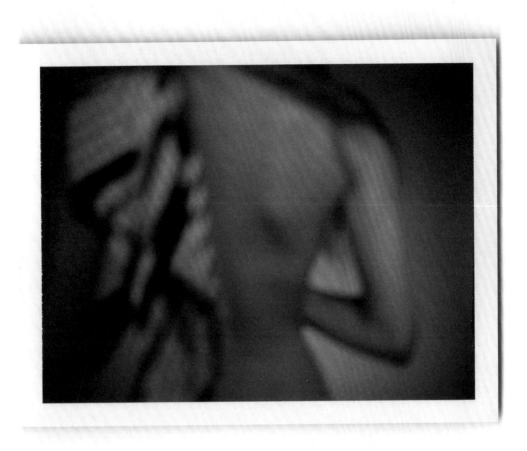

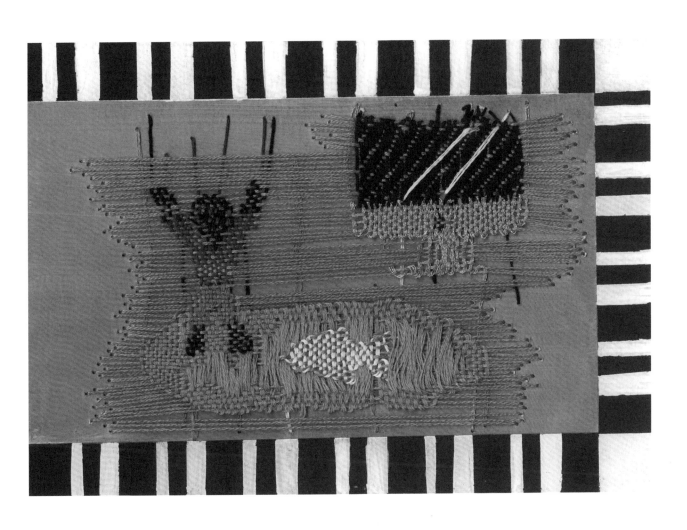

Hyderabad in Bangalore 03.31 am
`CONSTRUCTING THE IDEA`

11-08-16/01

LITT ANDALISM

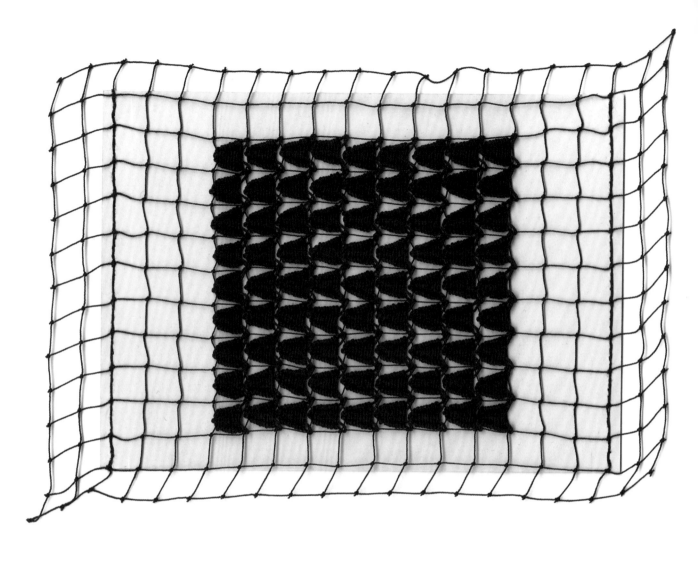

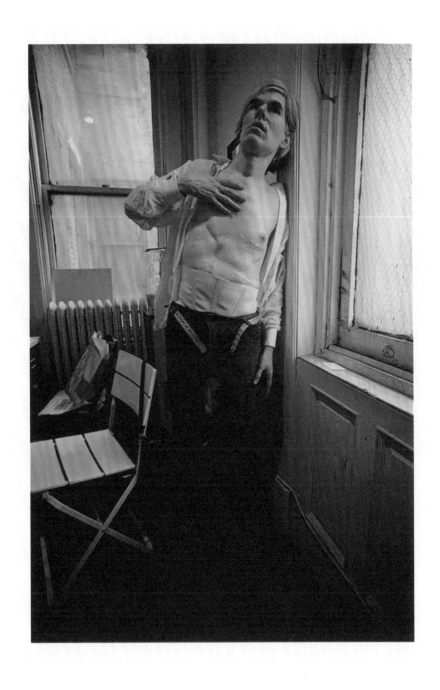

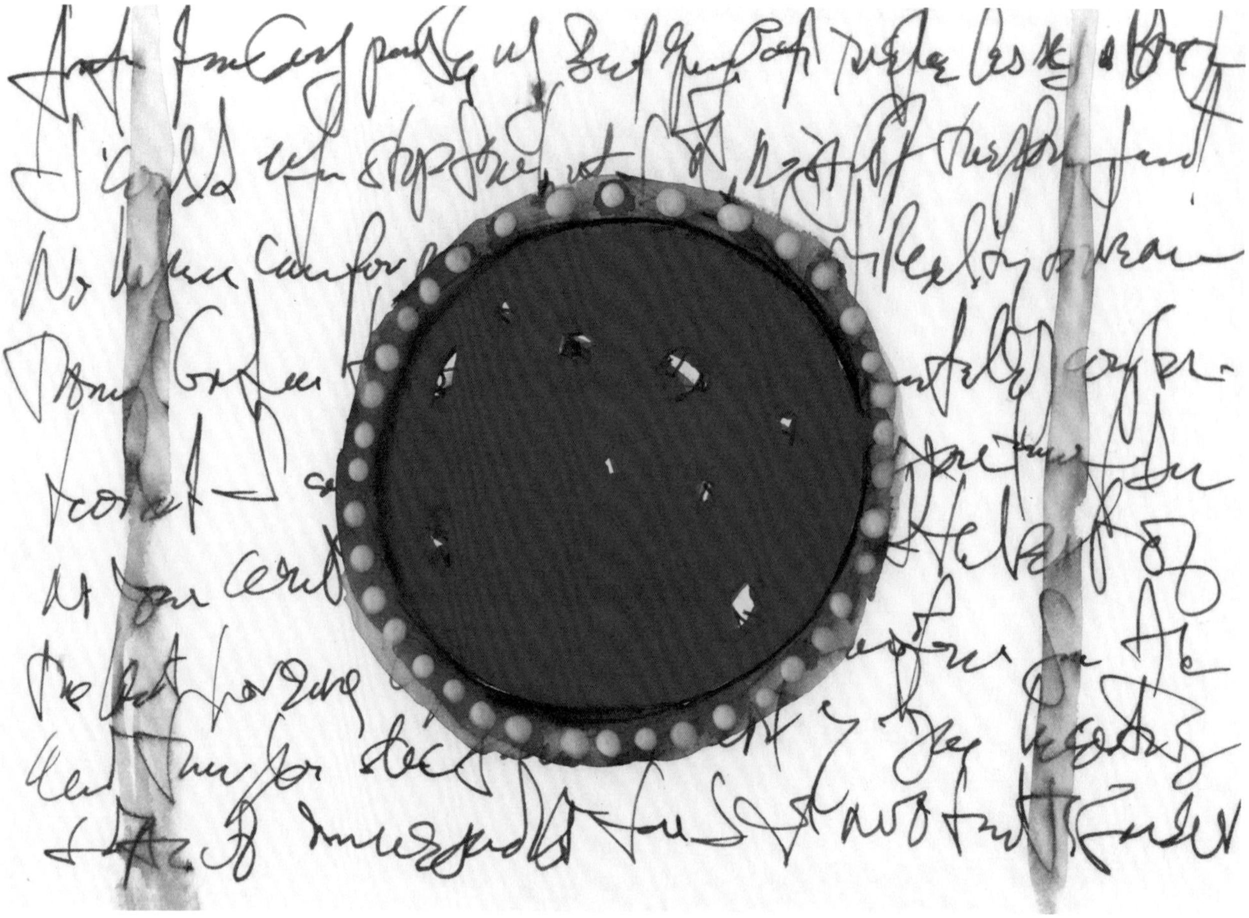

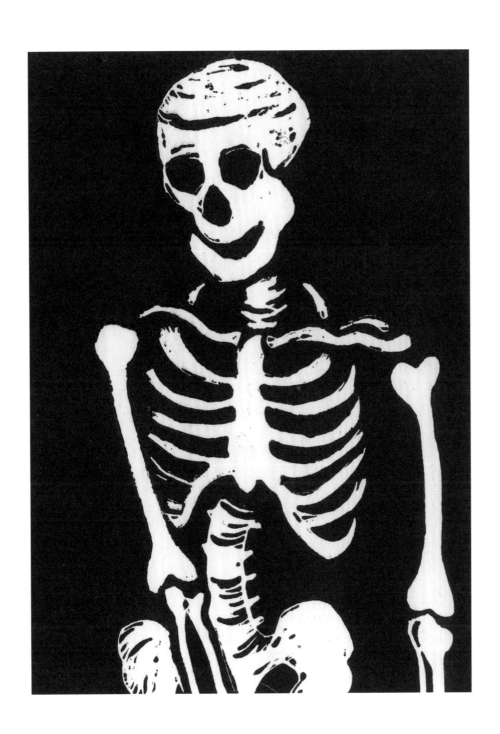

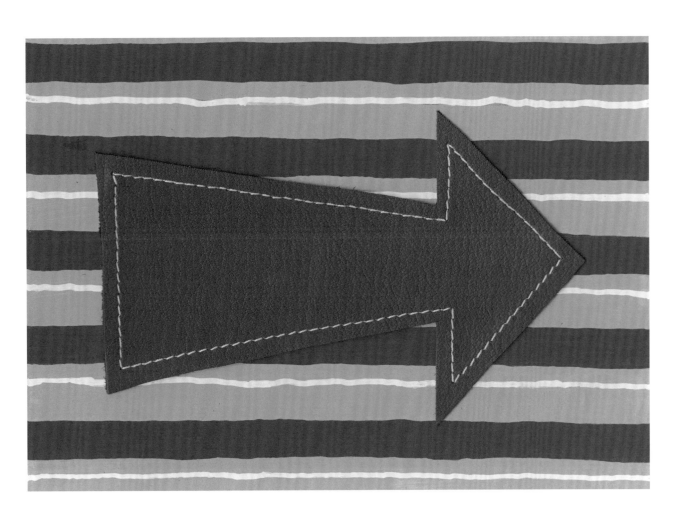

BOOM

Noomi

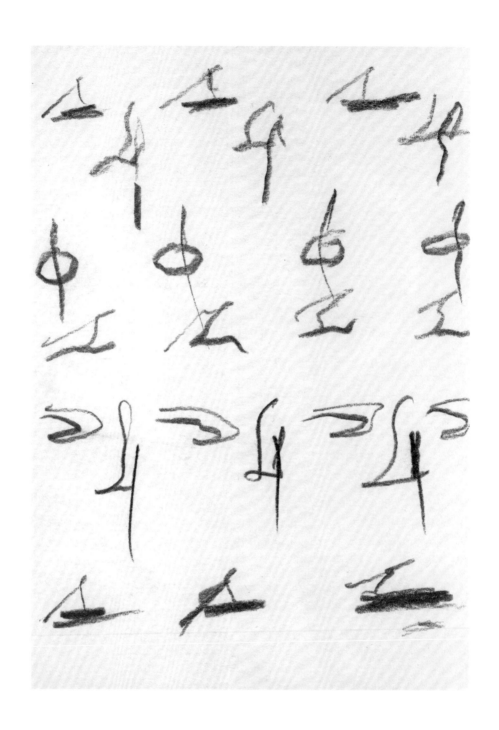

155

Jim Perdue, the chairman of Perdue Farms, has appeared in company ads for 20 years. The theme of new spots is "We believe in a better chicken."

there's a team behind the leader, making great things happen."

fed its chickens steroids or hormones, and never will. A disclaimer supering

Royal college of Art

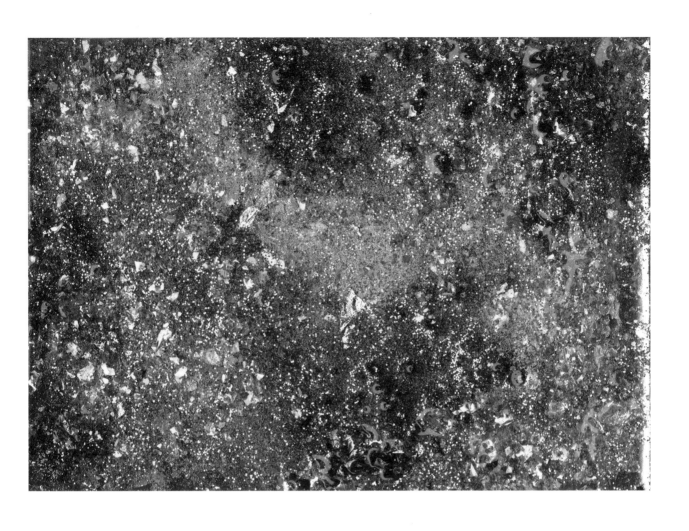

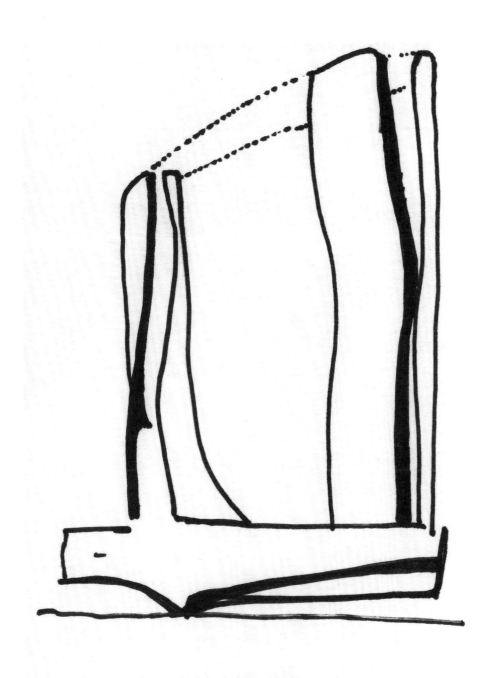

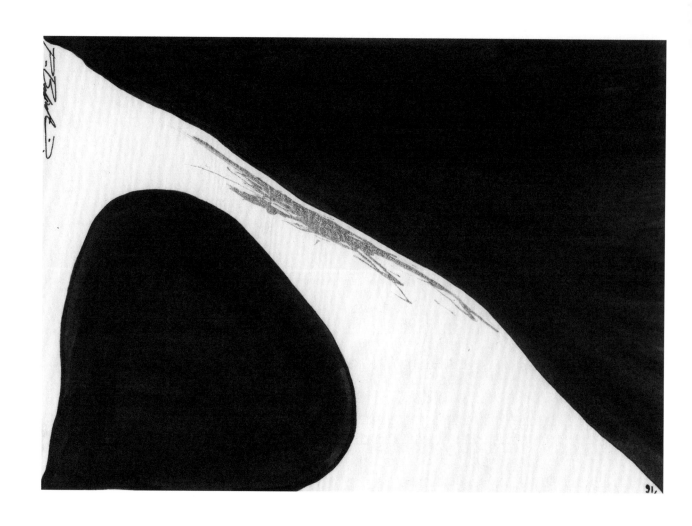

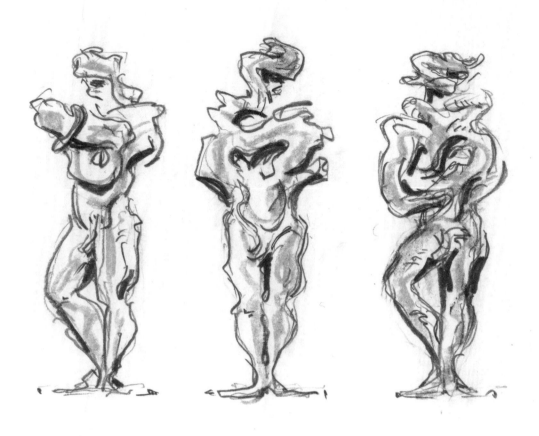

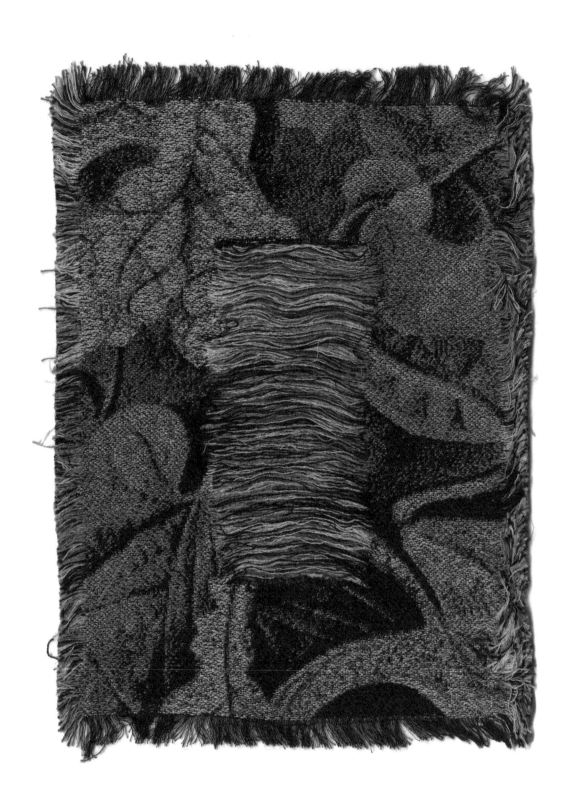

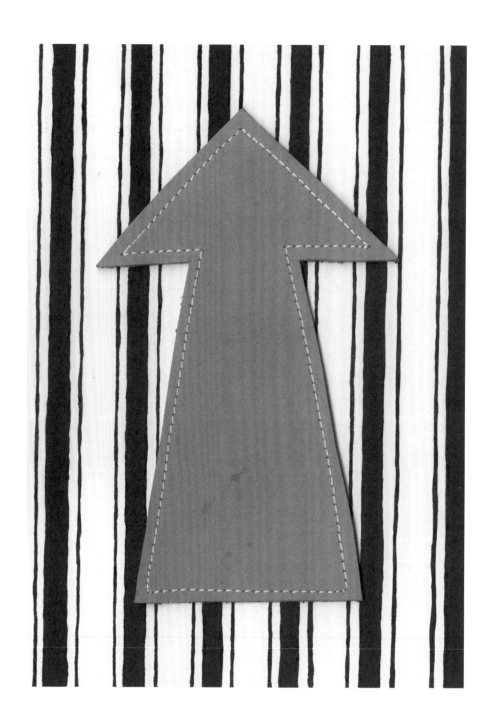

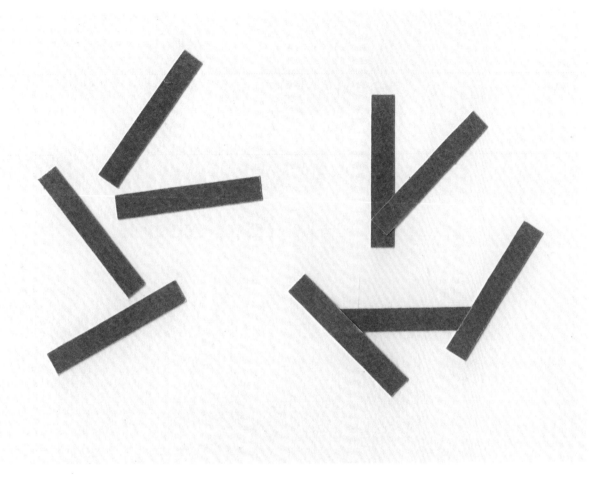

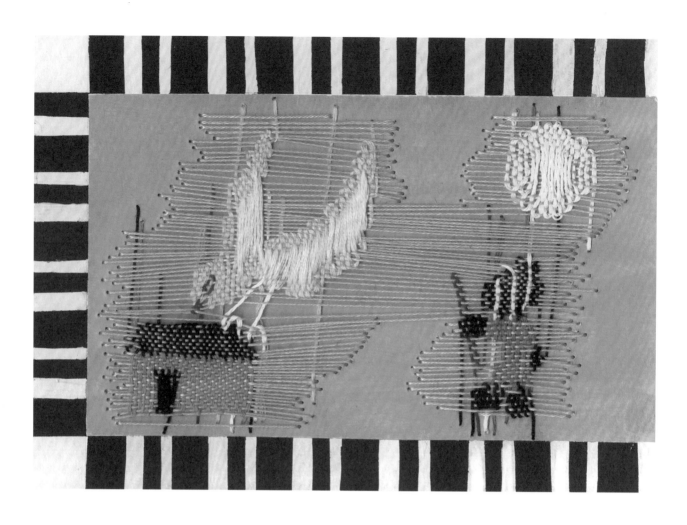

Architecture as Forest.

FLYBONE....

169   VICTOR CRUZ [AMERICAN FOOTBALL PLAYER]

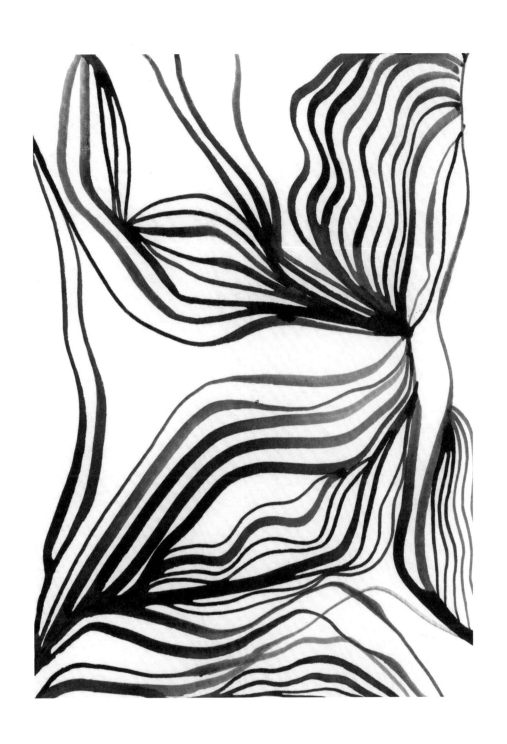

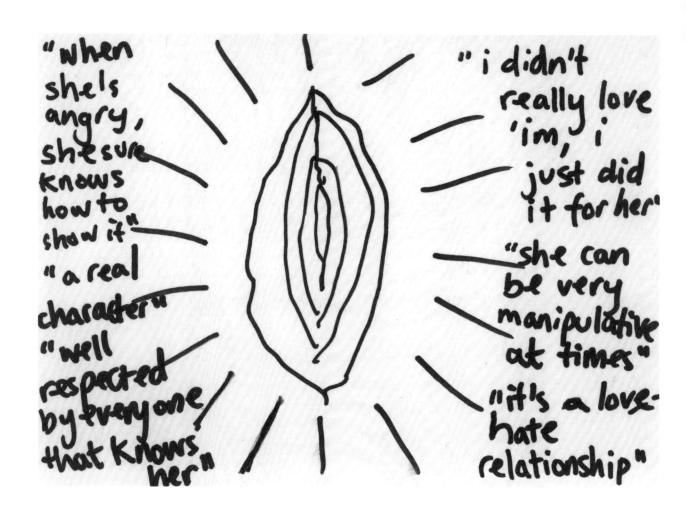

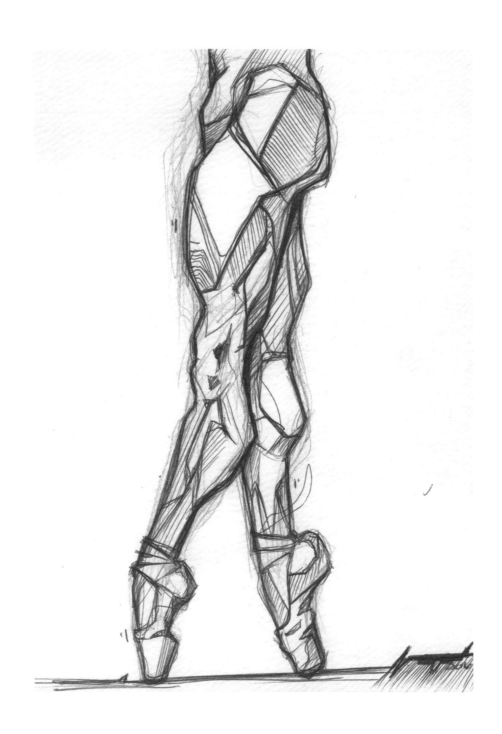

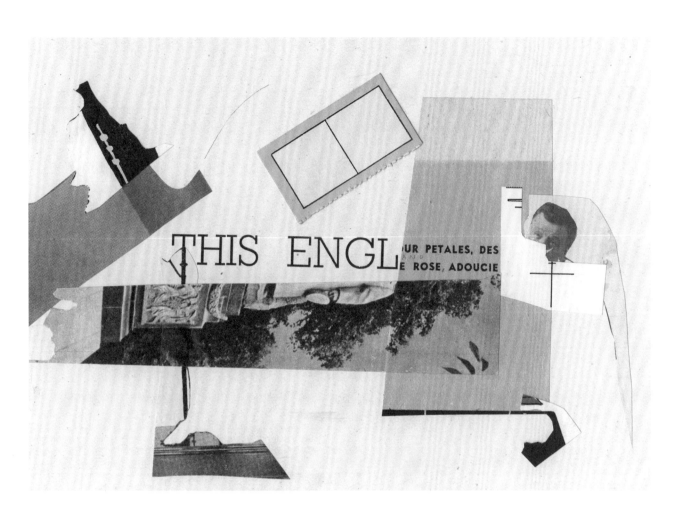

THIS ENGL   UR PETALES, DES
             E ROSE, ADOUCIE

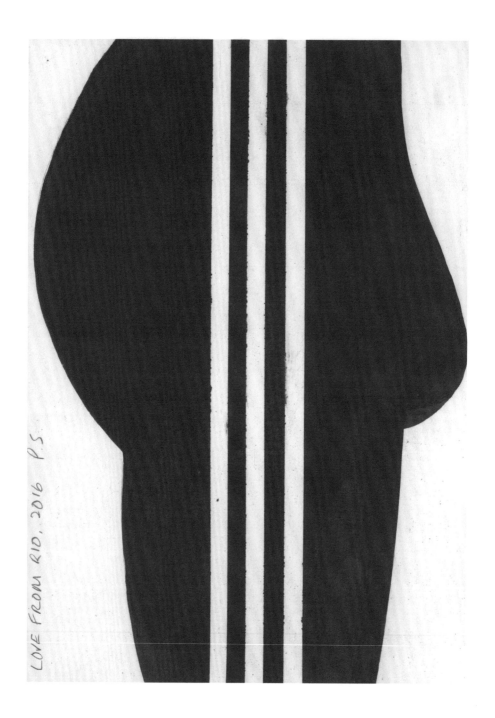

LOVE FROM RIO, 2016 P.S.

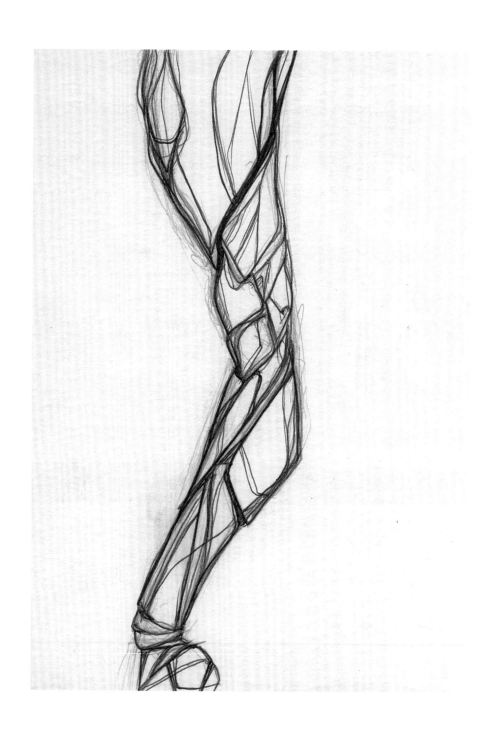

EX1: FILL IN WITH THE RIGHT COLORS

EX. 1: FILL IN THE RIGHT COLORS.

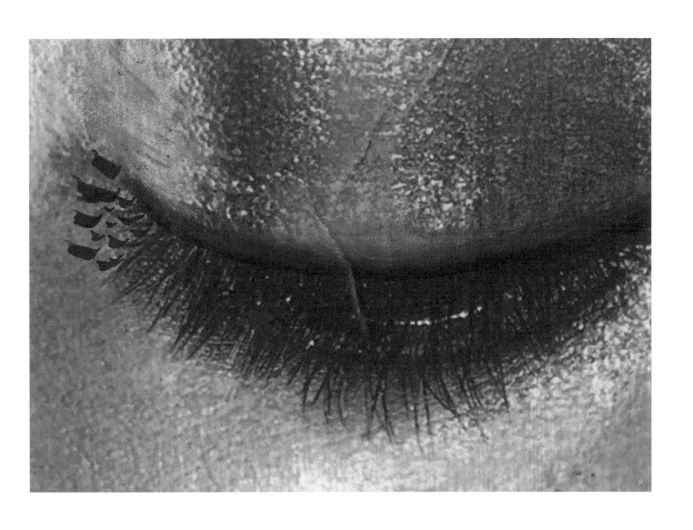

Architecture as Cloud.

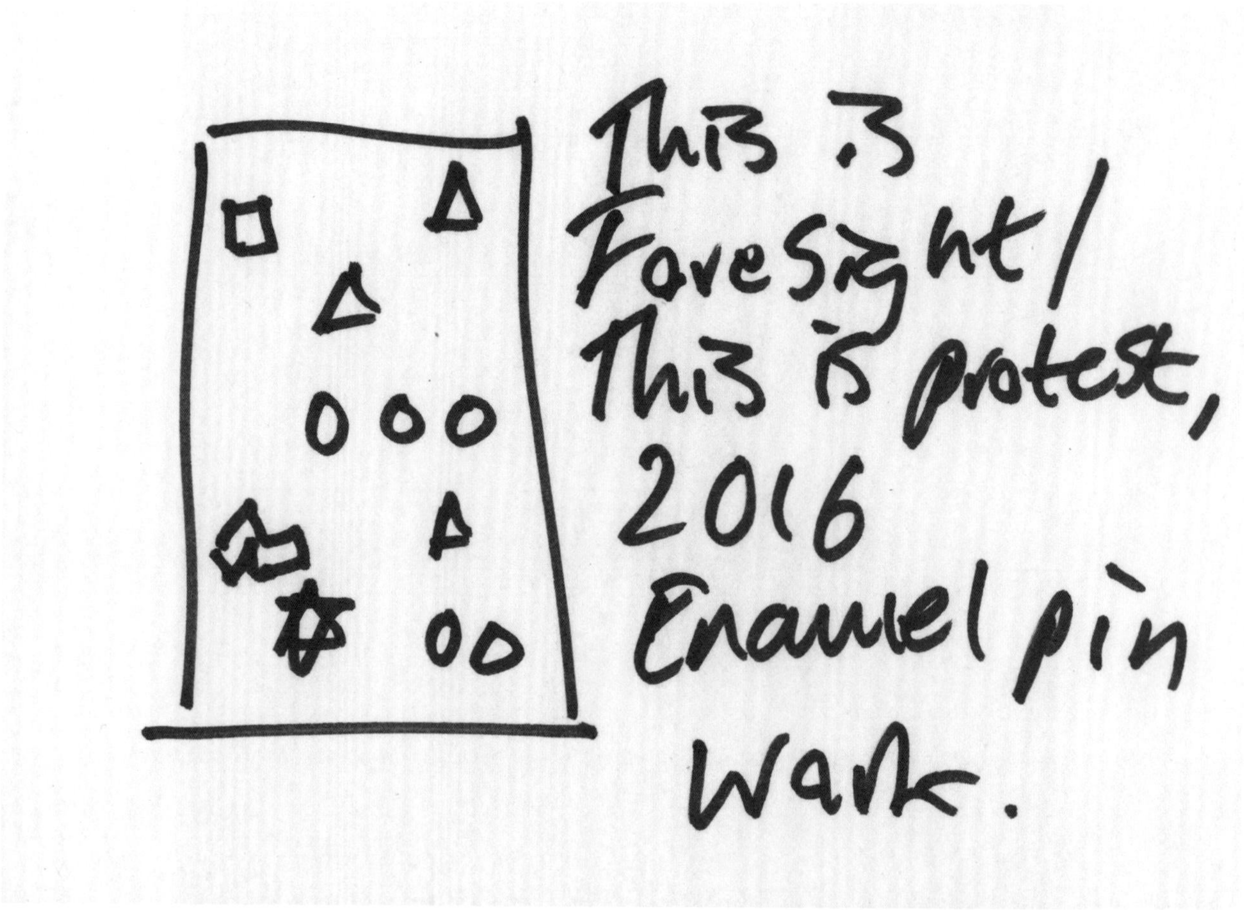

This is
Foresight/
This is protest,
2016
Enamel pin
work.

DEENA ALJUHANI ABDULAZIZ [EDITOR-IN-CHIEF AT VOGUE ARABIA]

"TC". 1993
PAINTING BY CHRIS MILTON

© CHRIS MILTON
TEL. 0769 580808

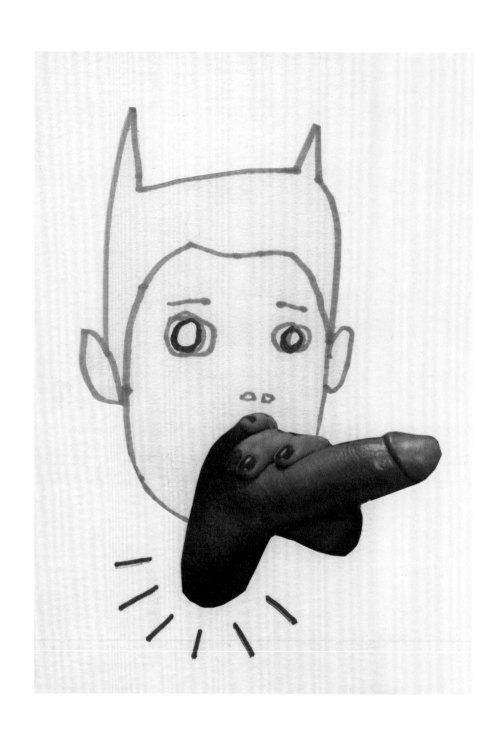

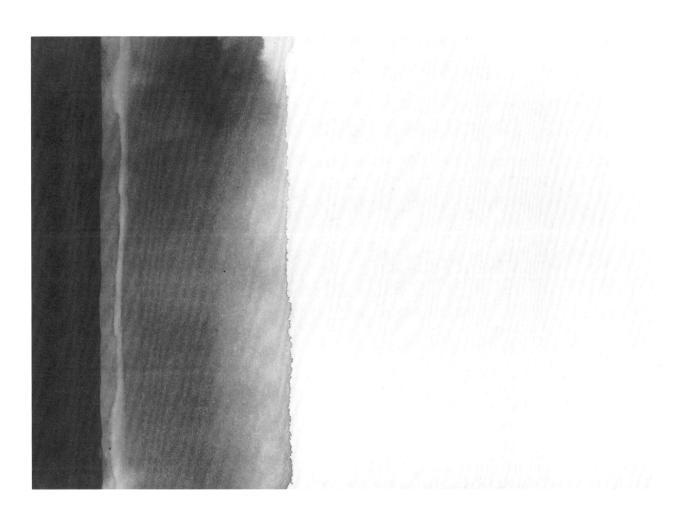

GB   X.

MY PLAN FOR THIS POLAROID WAS TO
SCAN IT & THEN BLOW IT UP HUGE..
LIKE 2M X 1.5M... THEN THE MORE
I LOOKED AT IT I THOUGHT IT WOULD
BE A BETTER PAINTING. EITHER WAY
THE COLORS & LINES TO BE FOUND BY
THE POOL @ THE STANDARD HOTEL IN
HOLLYWOOD ARE QUITE REMARKABLE!

August 21st

Dear Elsa,
    Remembering our
great summer together!
.... I have great news.
for you.... I've found
your EARRING under the
olive tree !!!
find it fixed with tape
at the back of the
postcard_
        Love, love, love D.

Elsa Merini
33, via Appia
00183 - Roma
ITALIA

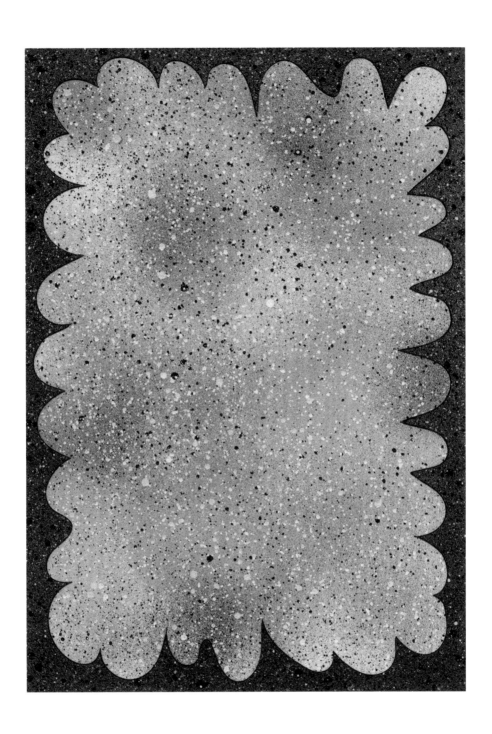

HELLO.

HELLO.

I WAS BRED TOO TAME

SLIE PLATT
PARTNER TO PLAY
ASTON
ERNEST
TITLE: Grants availible
in this area

DIASKU
TATTOO
TITLE: '6:22pm
etc blar blar blar'

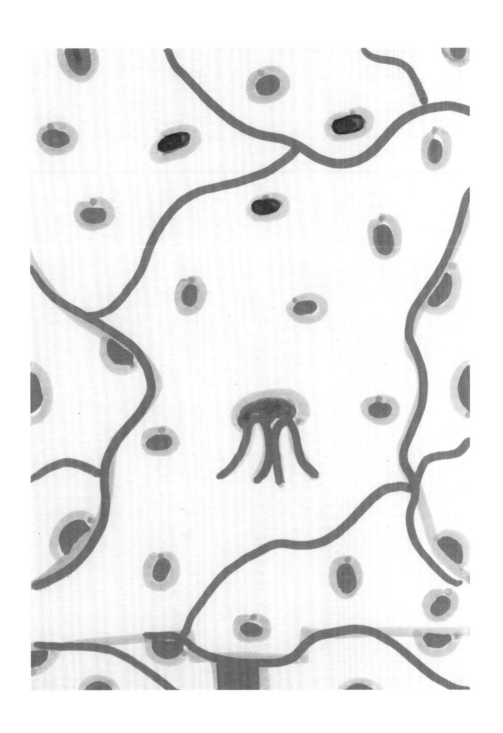

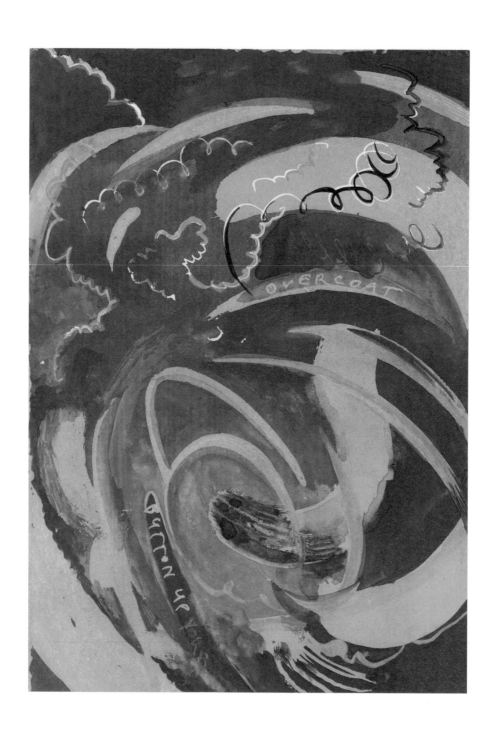

22:22

ANDREW CULLOO [RCA GRADUATE STUDENT AND RECIPIENT OF THE MONCLER SCHOLARSHIP]

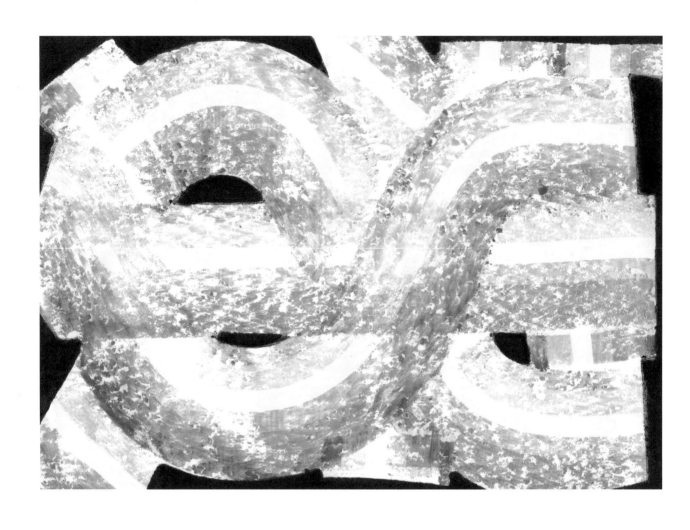

SCIASCIA GAMBACCINI [INTERNATIONAL EDITOR AT LARGE AT VANITY FAIR ITALIA]

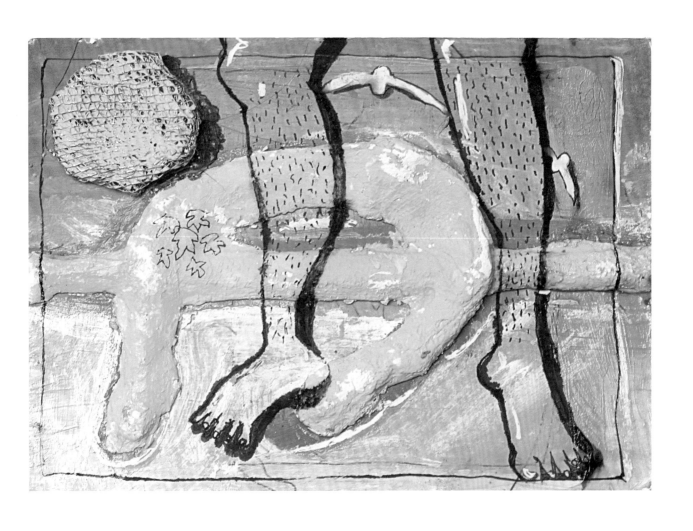

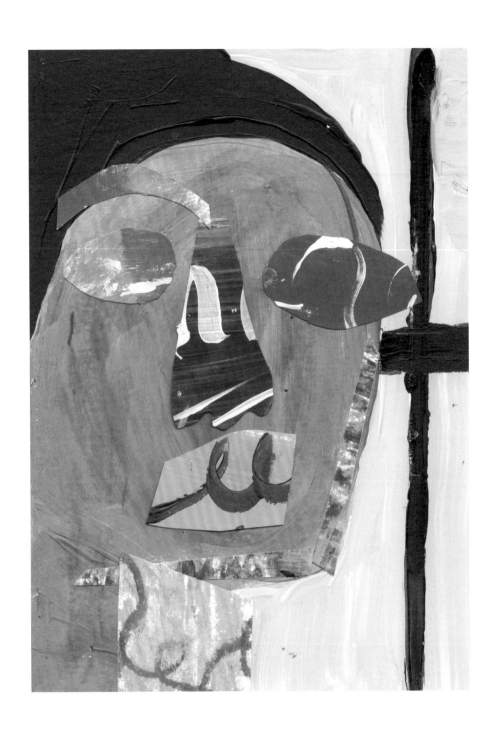

ARTHUR YATES [FASHION DESIGNER]

K2 VISTO DA NINA

I Know
let's start a
movement

HIKARI YOKOYAMA [CREATIVE CONSULTANT]

249   HIKARI YOKOYAMA [CREATIVE CONSULTANT]

WE ARE IN THIS TOGETHER.

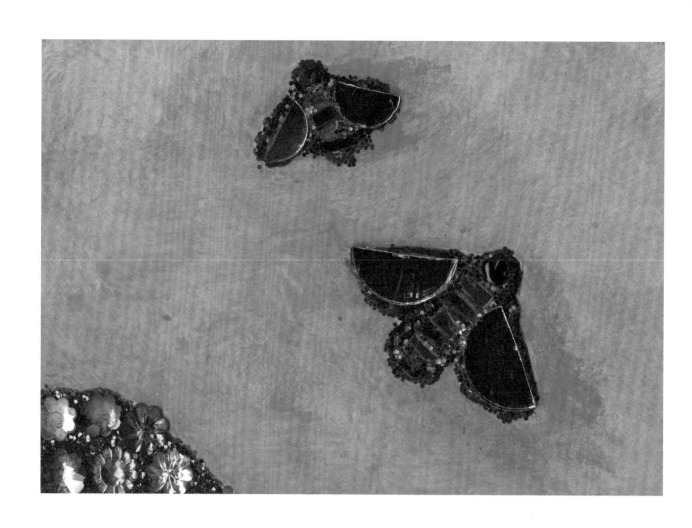

LUCK AND THE MYSTERY OF
PERSONALITY

↓

I SUPPOSE MOST OTHER
THINGS CAN BE ACCOUNTED FOR

↓

BUT NOT EVERYTHING
CAN BE MEASURED;
LIKE LOVE AND LUCK

AEIO NAEU FINNEGOISM

COLD HAPPY NIGHT 1927

LONDON → MILAN

LOVE CAN'T BE MEASURED

↓

IT'S AN INTANGIBLE THING

↓

DON'T (WELL, I WOULDN'T)
PUT TOO MUCH WEIGHT
ON IT

↓

RATHER, PLACE THE
EMPHASIS ON TRUST, PERHAPS

AE/O NHEU FUNK/D AMORALITY

I AM ON YOUR TEAM.

EIN UNVERGESSLICHER
MOMENT. . . . . . .

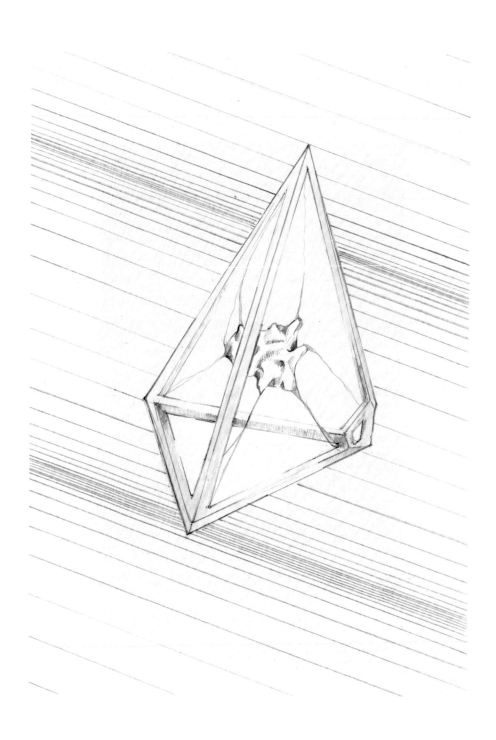

HENRY STANFORD [RCA GRADUATE STUDENT AND RECIPIENT OF THE MONCLER SCHOLARSHIP]

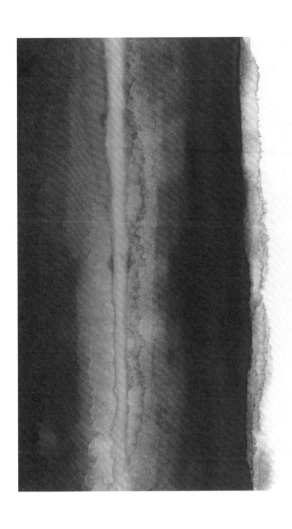

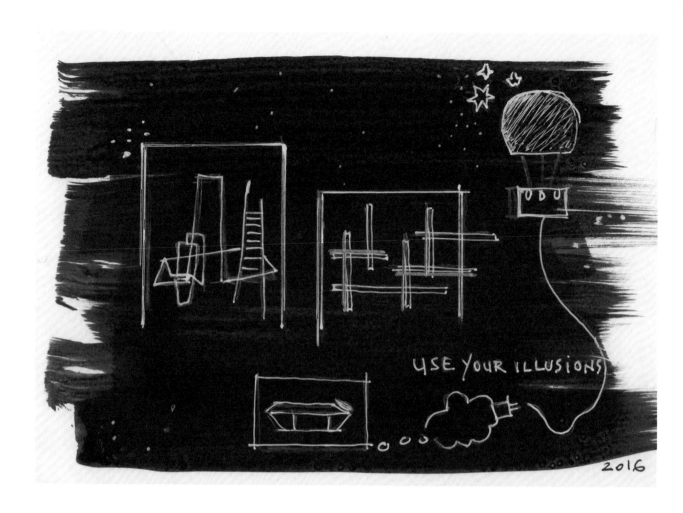

need to Dry

283   SHAUN MCDOWELL [ARTIST]

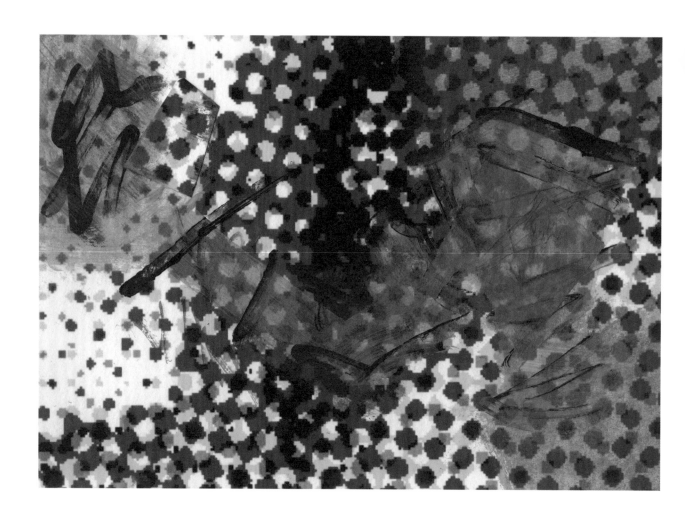

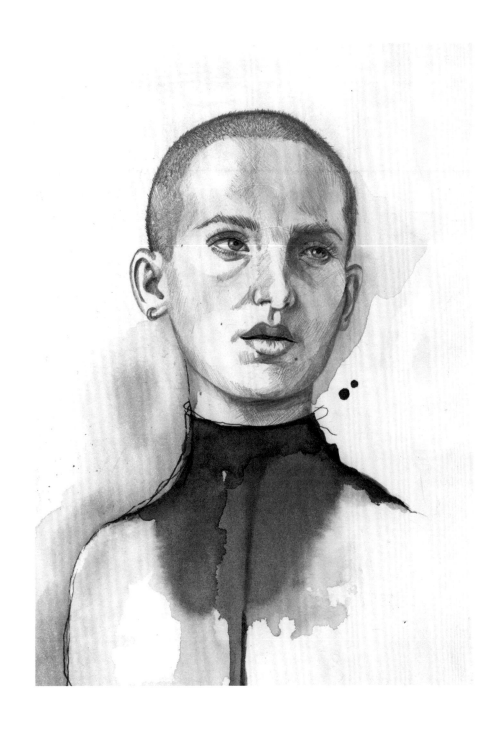

HANNA GARCIA FLEER FOR OFF WHITE C/O VIRGIL ABLOH™ [ARTIST]

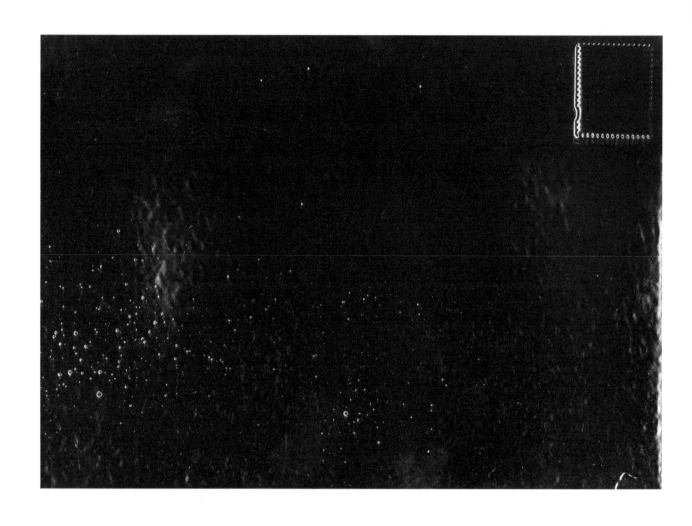

HANNA GARCIA FLEER FOR OFF WHITE C/O VIRGIL ABLOH™ [ARTIST]

GUILLAUME NERY [FRENCH FREEDIVER SPECIALIST]

EVERGREEN
ROOM AND
HINOKI OIL
TITLE: Romance
Languages.

TO DO:
_____

. LIVE IN
THE
MOMENT

EMILY JOHNSTON [BLOGGER AND SOCIALITE]

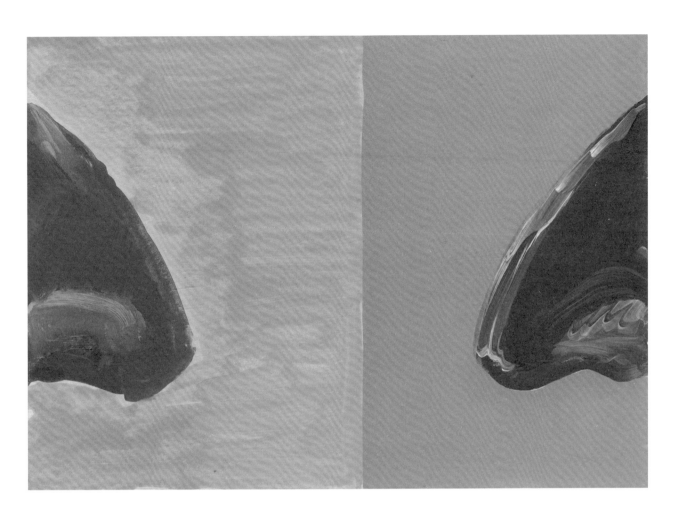

DESTROY ME
DESTROY ME SO I CAN BECOME MY TRUE ME
DESTROY ME AND SET ME FREE
DESTROY ME BUT DONT KILL ME
I'M TO HARD TO LOVE
I'M TO HARD TO FEEL LOVE
PLEASE DESTROY ME SO I CAN START AGAIN.

NOOMI

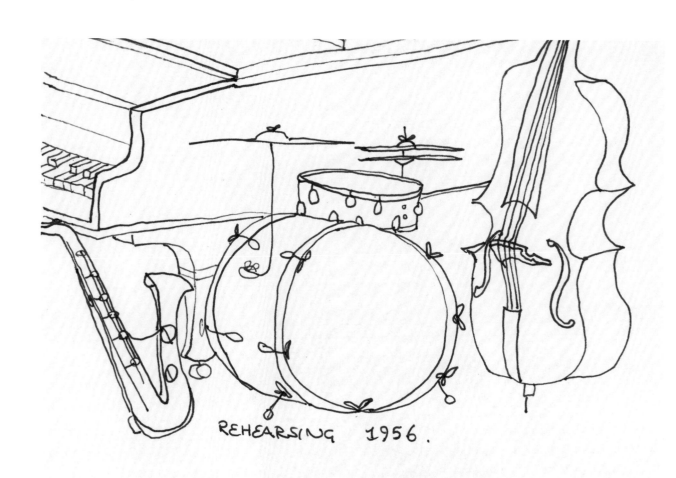

REHEARSING 1956.

USE YOUR ILLUSIONS

2016

holiday season

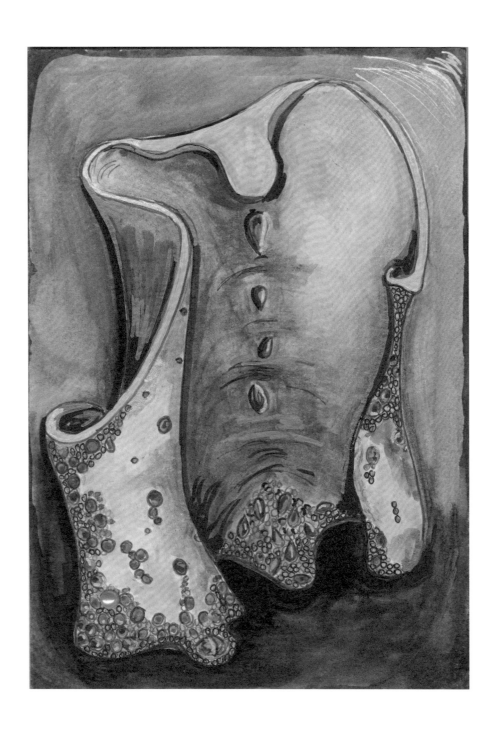

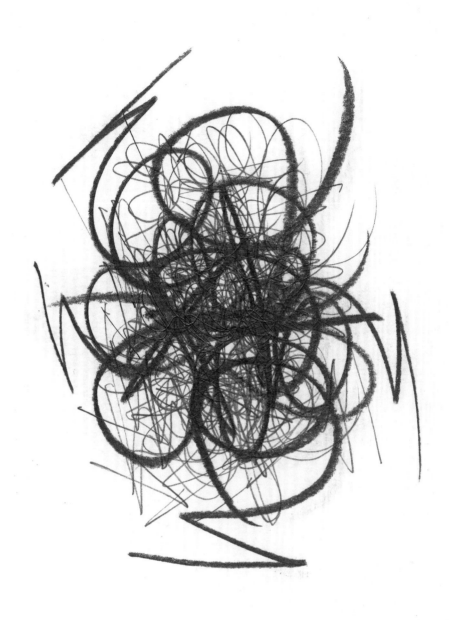

HAPPY ASHLEY

CELEBRATE AND HAVE A GOOD TIME!
my heart belongs to ELVIS PResley
bath time
Velocity
subscribe
Dream boat
S.O.S
H.M.S
Golden girl
Zuburbz
NO HASSLE
coca-cola
PLASTIC SURGERY
moon walker
LAST CHANCE TO ESCAPE PLANET EARTH
improve your image, be seen with me
Bad Mood
TAZER
Extra terrestrial
pireced ears
bambini
First born
dream alliance
RV MARRIED?
I ♥ GIRLS
I ♥ BOYS
HAIRCUT

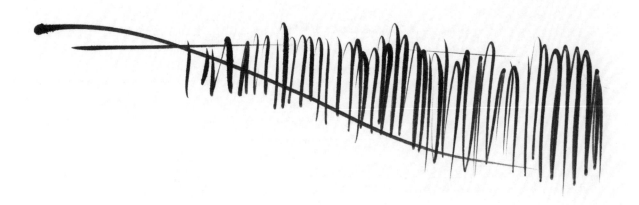

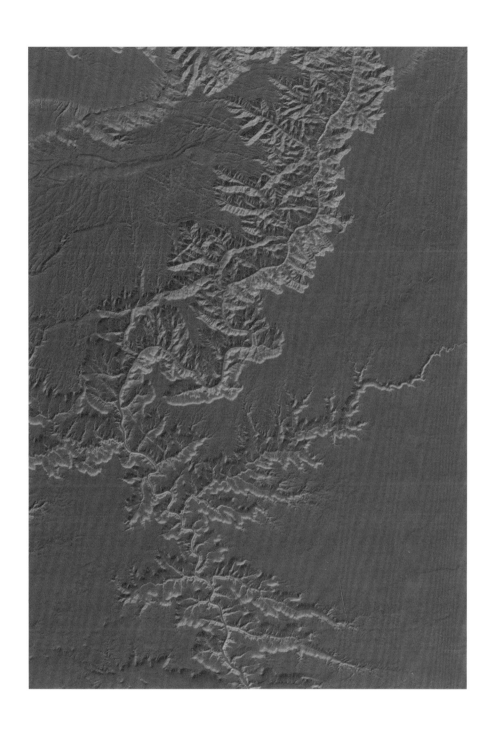

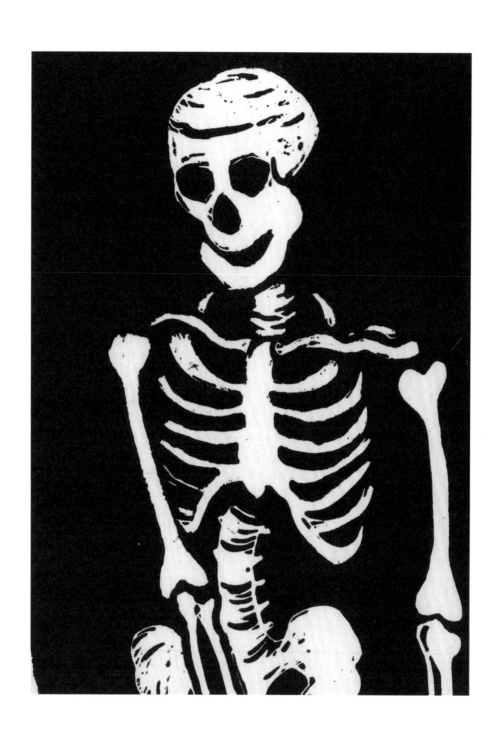

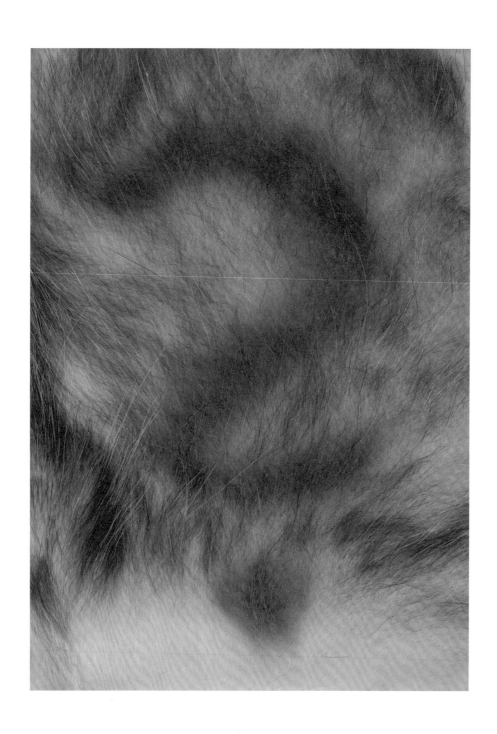

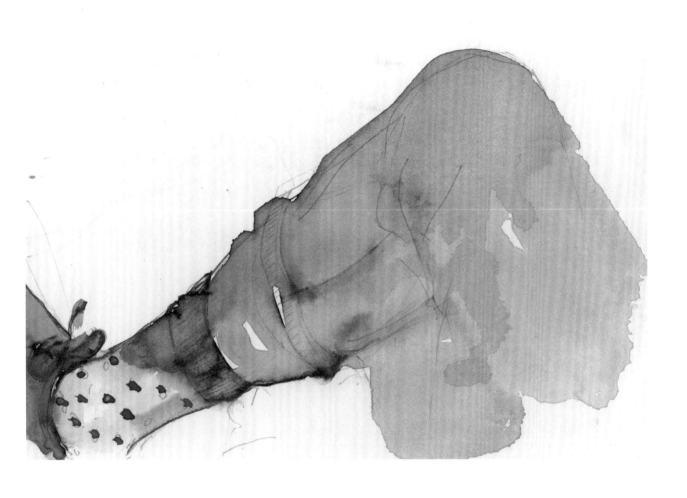

338   RUPERT THOMAS [EDITOR AT THE WORLD OF INTERIORS]

MONEY FOR THE LANDLORD
£432.46 – rent
£50 – new contract

FUCK!

I think you have to be rich to make it as a model.

School just feels like a bad dream now ...

I've moved in! On the fridge downstairs it says "Some people are gay, get over it."

Oyster card

£25

ENDLESSLY!

if it's Greek it's =

CONFUSING.

... and I'm moving

TO LONDON!!

I'M NOT SURE WHERE I'M SLEEPING TONIGHT?

I hope I get the bus!

Saw a guy wanking (NOT you)

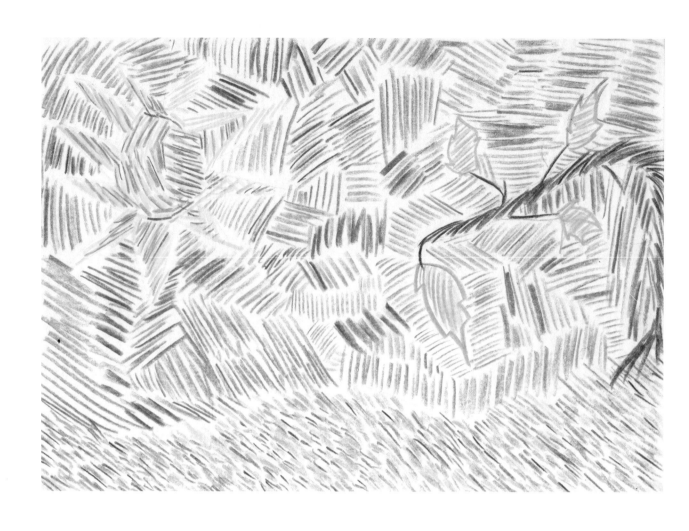

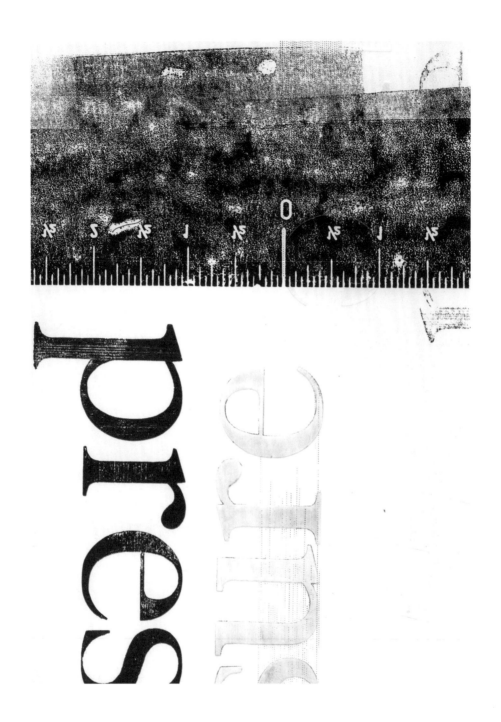

TONY CHAMBERS [EDITOR-IN-CHIEF OF WALLPAPER*]

RICCARDO POZZOLI [CO-FOUNDER & CEO AT TBS CREW]

EVA CAVALLI DÜRINGER [DESIGNER]

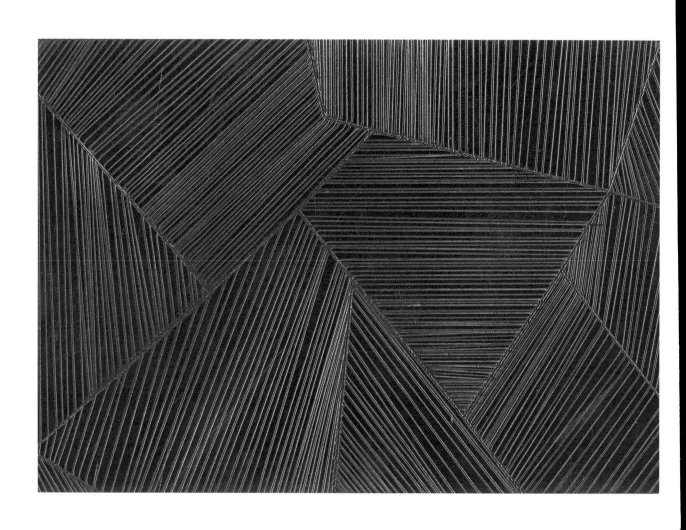

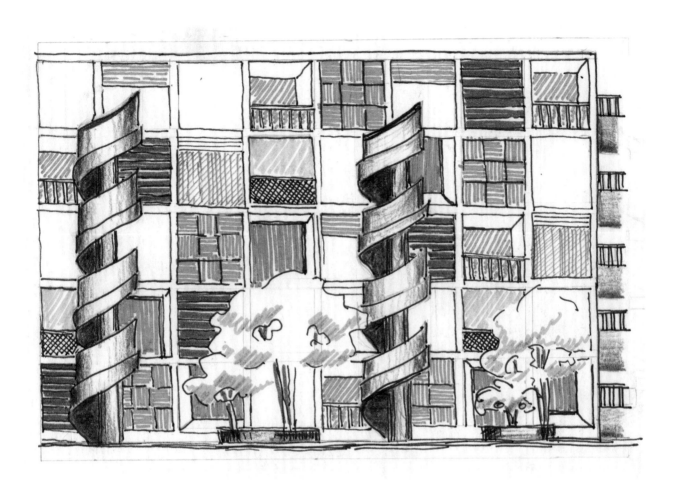

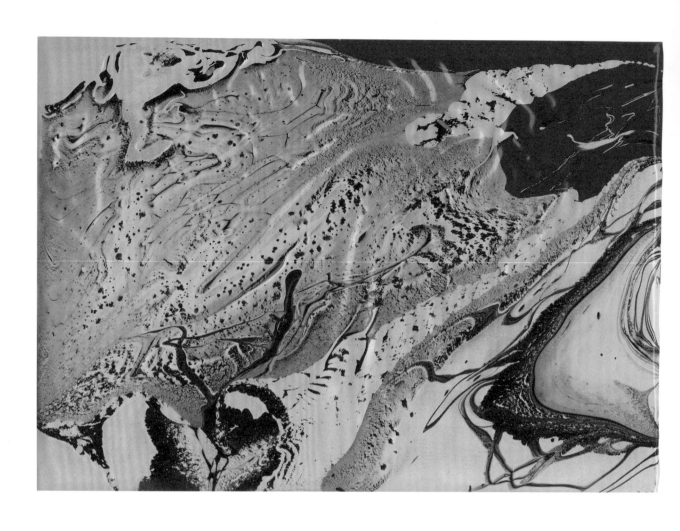

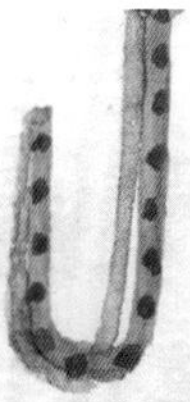

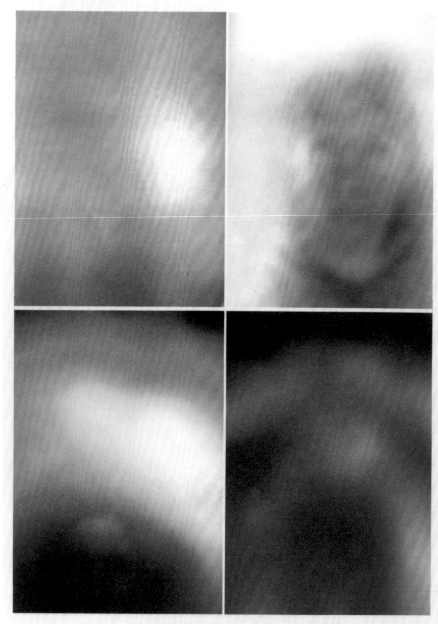

Study for "The Self in the Digital Age"

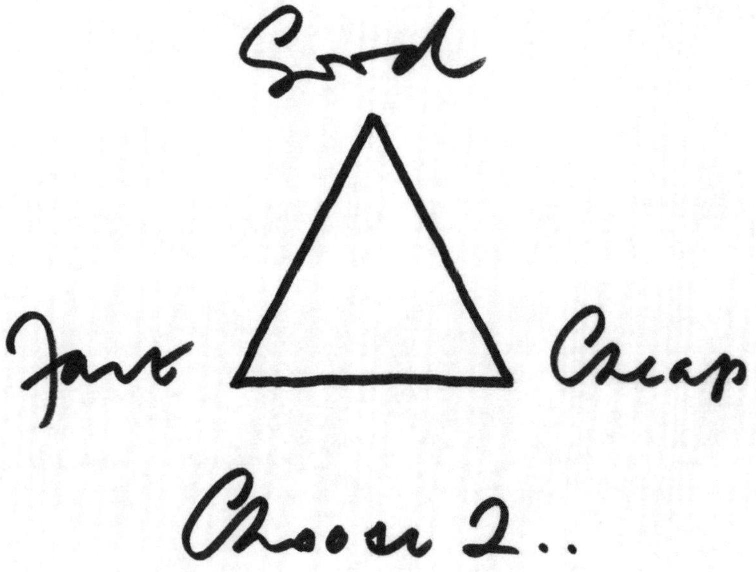
Good
Fast
Cheap
Choose 2..

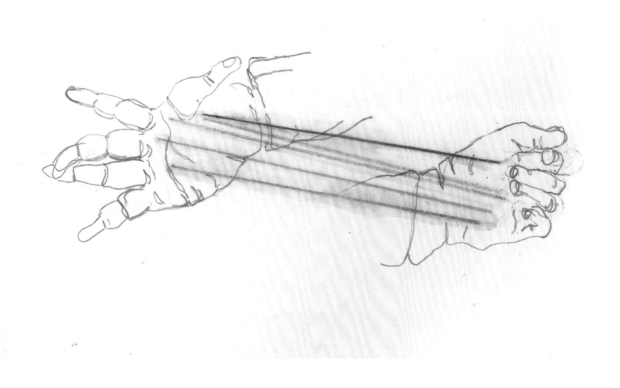

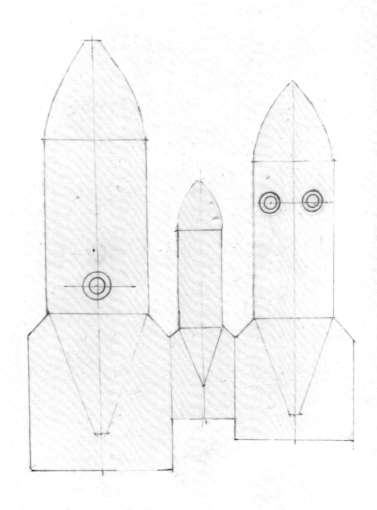

NOT BY
ANYBODY
IMPORTANT
(SORRY)

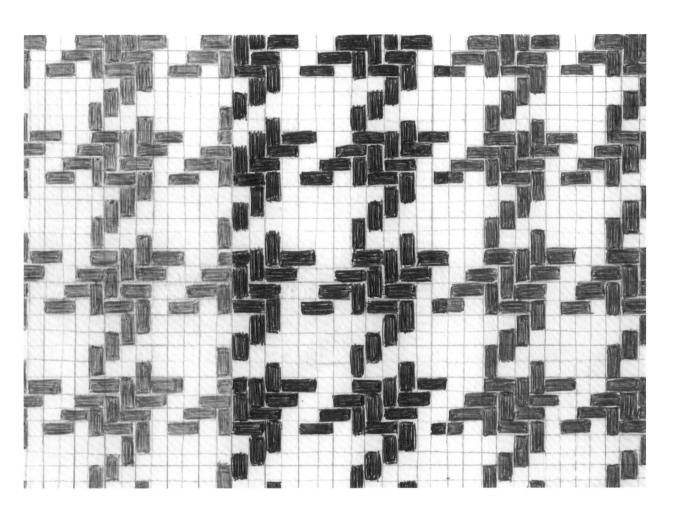

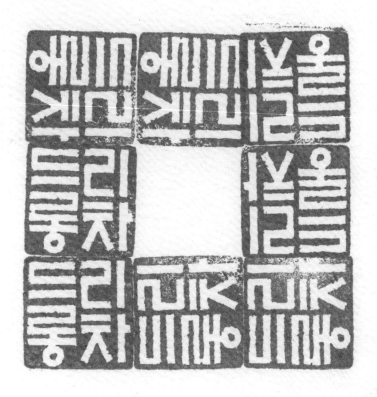

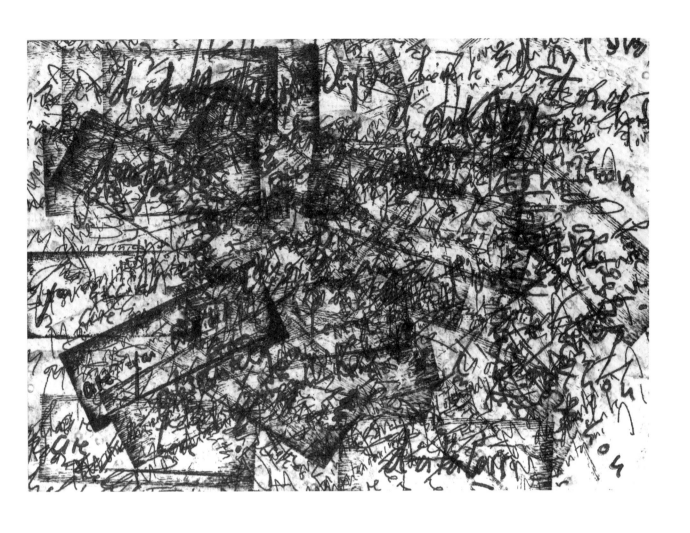

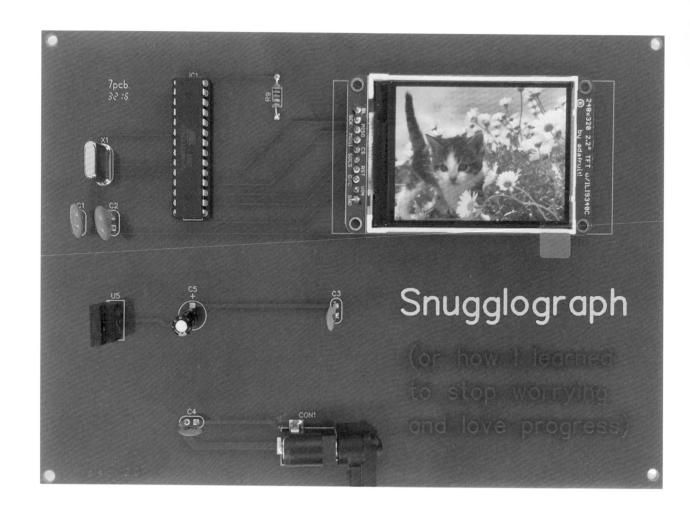

Snugglograph

(or how I learned to stop worrying and love progress)

JOHN BALDESSARI [ARTIST]

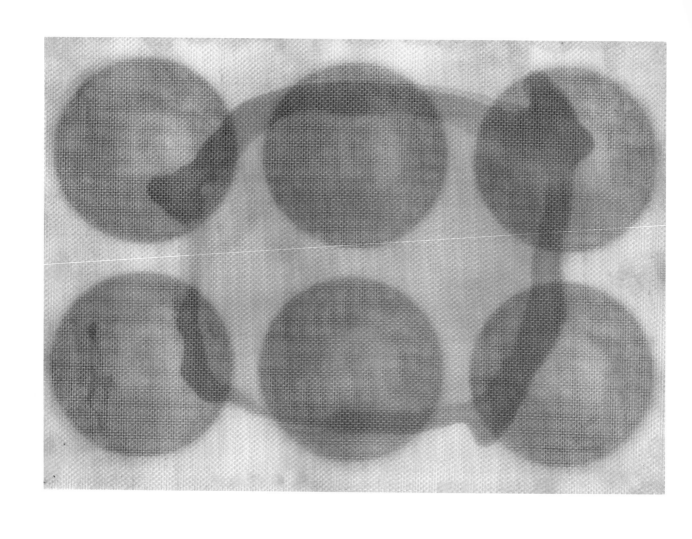

DAN COLEN, NYC, 2008

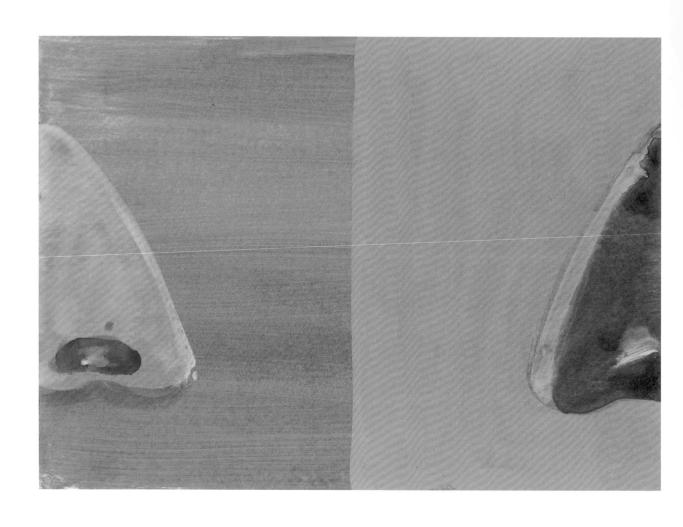

"FIGHTER HAWK"
mechanical bird hybrid
metal / feathers

Love !

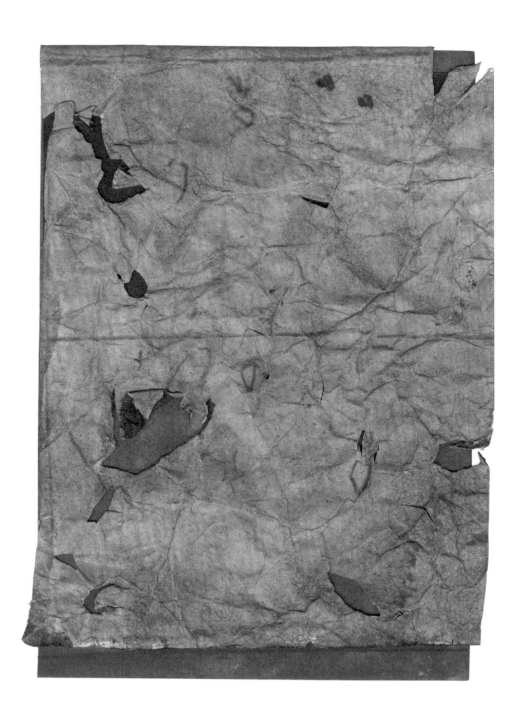

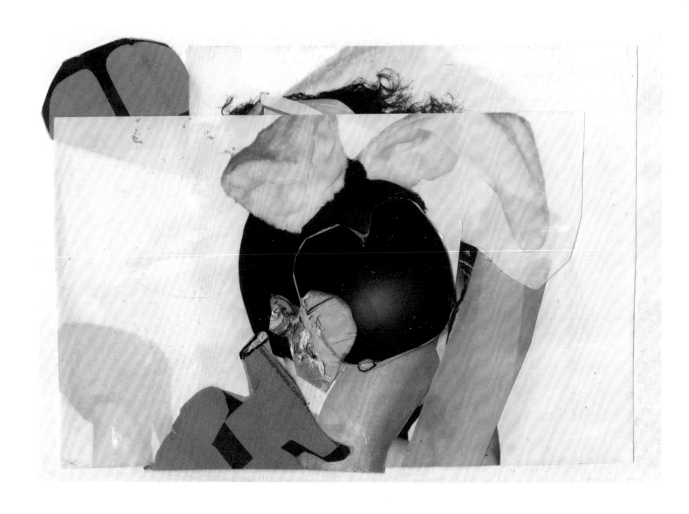

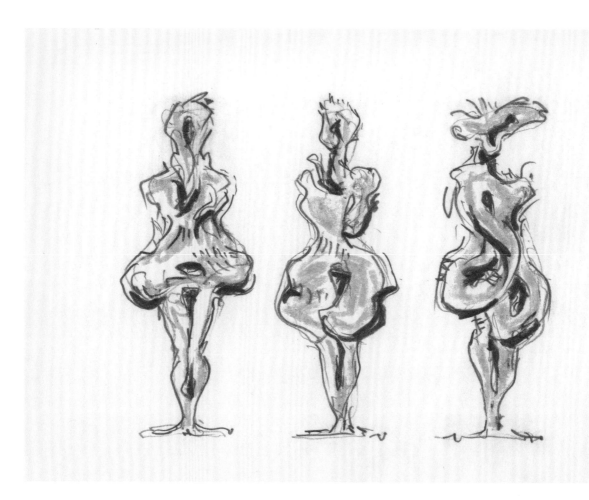

THESE THINGS WERE WRITTEN in the BIBLE, the QUran, &

on the WALLS OF EGYPTIAN AND ROMAN BUILDING

THESE thing WERE WRITTEN ABOUT

the KINGS & QUEENS that

HAVE COME & GONE. ABOUT

GREAT MEN ABOUT POETS & ABOUT

KILLERS. ALL these things

that HAPPENED HAVE Meaning EVERYthing

that HAPPENS SERVES into

EACH other. these things

WERE

ALL MEANT TO HAPPEN.

-THERE's A MEANING to LiFE.

— NASIR BIN OLU DARA JONES —

Life is a stage.... Set to be swept away.
J.G. Ballard.

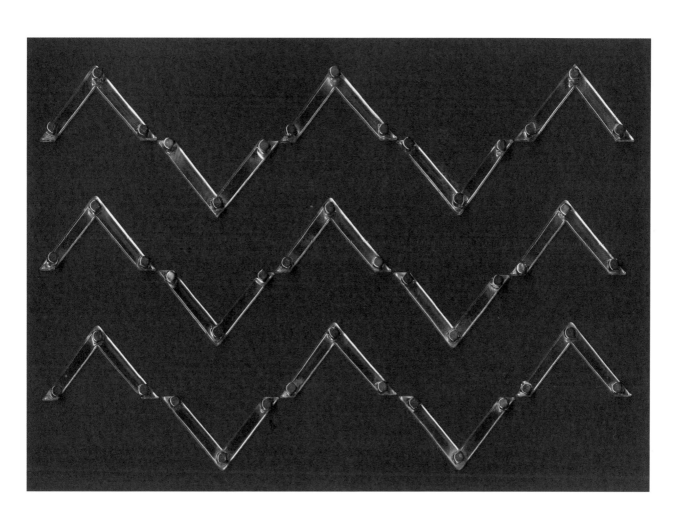

NORFOLK 16

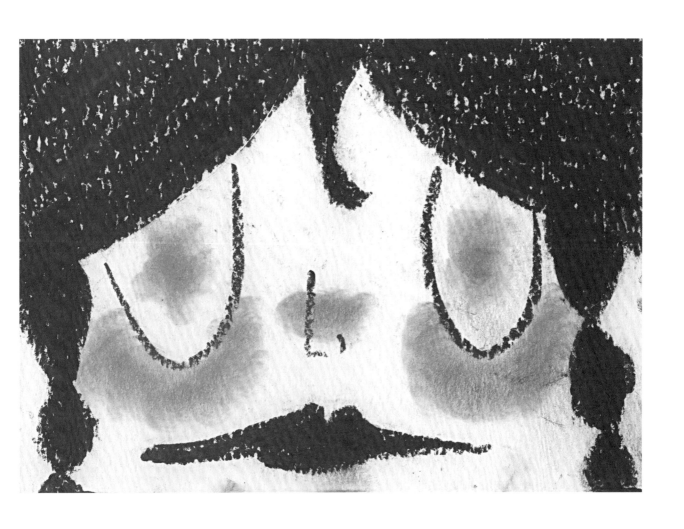

426   PETITE MELLER [SINGER]

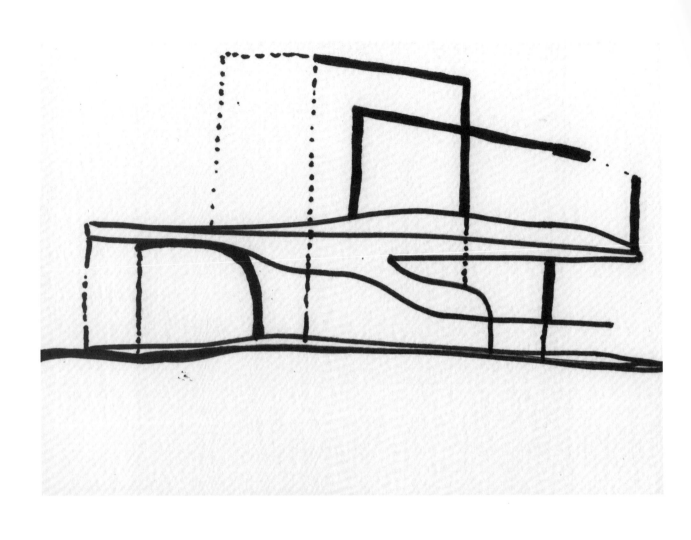

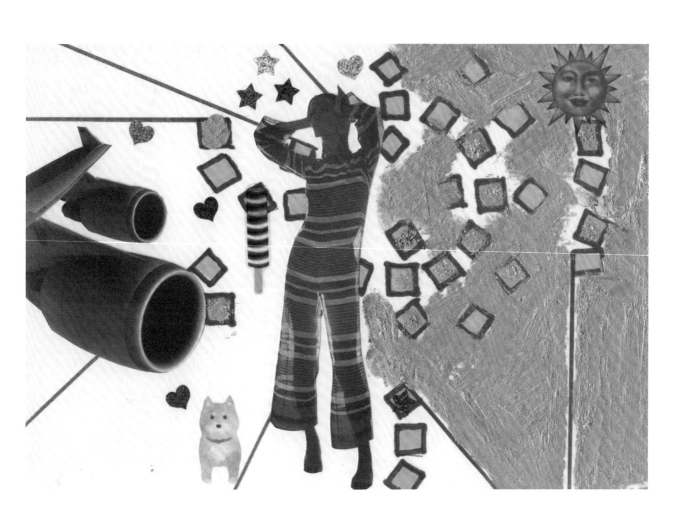

"FIGHTER HAWK"
mechanical bird hybrid
metal / feathers

MY SUPERIORITY
COMPLEX IS

BETTER

THAN

YOURS.

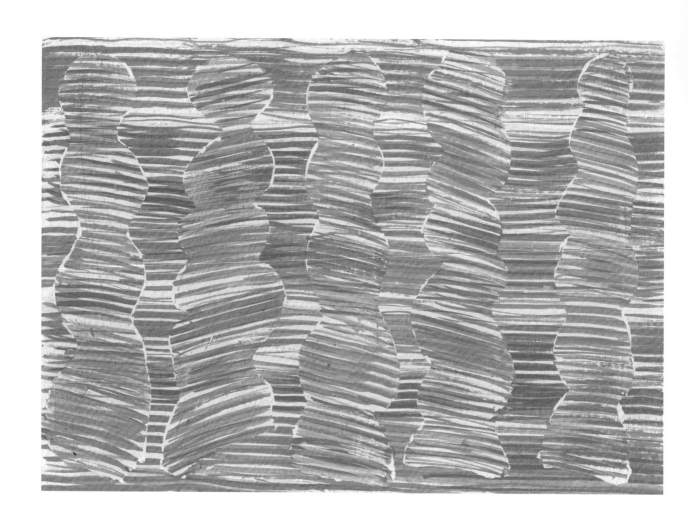

MOBILE DRAWING STUDIO

447   IOURI PODLADTCHIKOV [PROFESSIONAL SNOWBOARDER]

449 FRANCA SOZZANI [EDITOR-IN-CHIEF OF VOGUE ITALIA]

OUR HOLY HOUSE

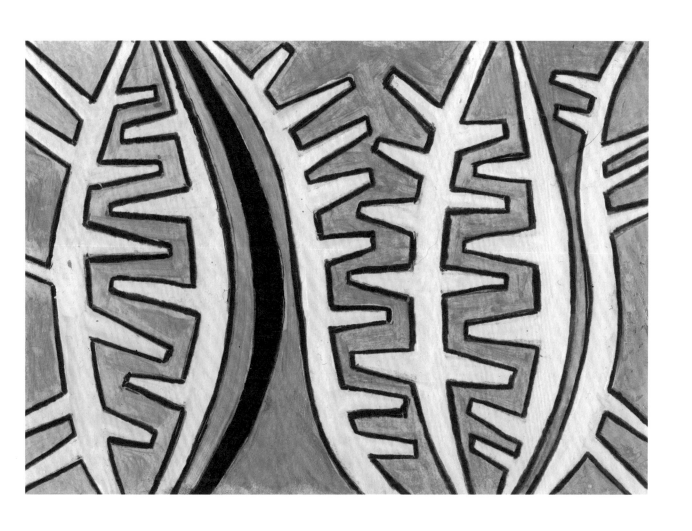

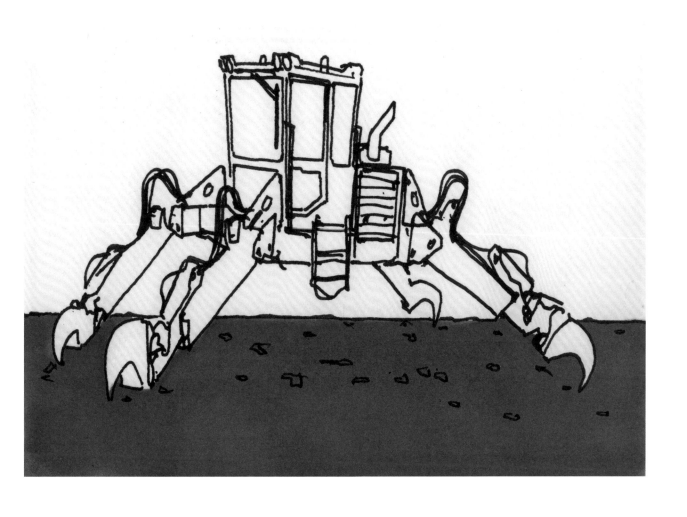

smackeroony!

cheers, sweetie *

darlings..

Kissy,
Kissy!

Be fab forever—
xx

Joanna Lumley

mwah!

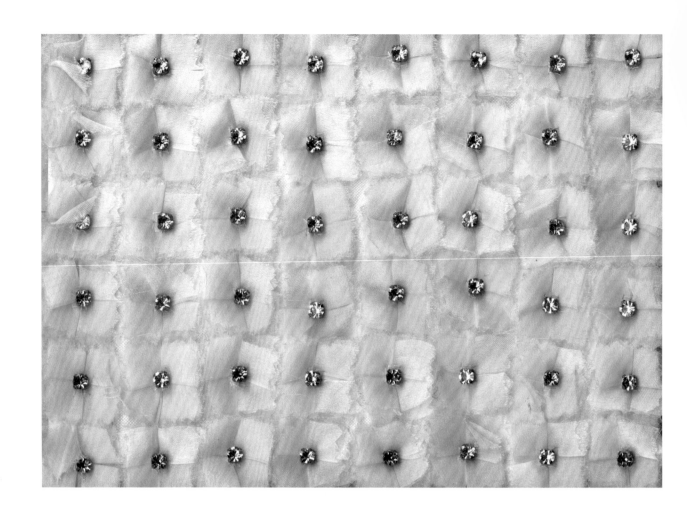

ASHLEY HEATH [EDITOR-IN-CHIEF OF POP MAGAZINE]

THANK YOU TO EVERYONE
WHO HAS MADE THIS BOOK POSSIBLE:

ROYAL COLLEGE OF ART
AND ITS RECTOR PAUL THOMPSON

NANCY OAKLEY [PURPLE]

TIM BLANKS

ARTISTS

MARY GREENWELL
AA BRONSON
SINK THE PINK
TATA SURGULADZE
SIMON LEAHY-CLARK
SADIE WILLIAMS
NICK HORNBY
REBECCA WARD
DAVE BENETT
JONATHAN SCHOFIELD
GARTH LEWIS
LUKE EDWARD HALL
JOAN HECKTERMANN
ALLEGRA HICKS
LAPO ELKANN
MATTEO CECCARINI
SIMON RAWLINGS
[DAVID COLLINS STUDIO]
GIANLUCA LONGO
MADELON VRIESENDORP
JOSHUA CITARELLA
TOBIT ROCHE
THEBEARDSALAD
GILL BUTTON
ETEL ADNAN
EUDON CHOI
ERIC UNDERWOOD
CELIA BIRTWELL
OLGA VILSHENKO
JOSH OLINS
FLORIAN MEACCI
ELIZABETH STEWART
CHAOS FASHION
[CHARLOTTE STOCKDALE & KATIE LYALL]
MOLLY GODDARD
FAUSTINE STEINMETZ
CHRIS MARTIN
AMANDA HARLECH
SIMON EMMETT
GIOSETTA FIORONI
GIANLUCA CANTARO & DEE LEE
CLYM EVERNDEN
CARLO CRACCO
DAISY DE VILLENEUVE
OLIVIA MUNN
PETER BELL
JEAN PIGOZZI
GARY CARD
CHARLES JEFFREY

SALLY MUIR
DAN HOLDSWORTH
LAWRENCE WEINER
GILES DEACON
ANDREW ARTHUR
CAMILLA ÅKRANS
EDGARDO OSORIO
MICHELE PONTRANDOLFO
NATASHA SURGULADZE
SAM MCKNIGHT
SCARLETT CARLOS CLARKE
ALBERTO BIANI
EMMA GREENHILL
LUCA STOPPINI
CATHY LOMAX
JOHN TARGON
RIO URIBE
DAVID MONTGOMERY
PETER LINDBERGH
JUDY BLAME
NICK GRIMSHAW
SUSANNAH GARROD
CHRISTOPHER LE BRUN
JAMIE CAMPBELL BOWER
CHRIS BROOKS
ALEXANDER LEWIS
ALDO CIBIC
FLAVIE AUDI
BARNABY BARFORD
CARL TURNER
PRZEMEK PYSZCZEK
NICK FARHI
HOLLY JOHNSON
BENJAMIN SEIDLER
RYAN GANDER
JEANNE GANG
DAVID BAILEY
KENNETH TOPP
GIULIA GARBIN
LARRY BELL
JUDE LAW
IOURI PODLADTCHIKOV
JORDAN ASKILL
MICHAEL LINDSAY-HOGG
JOE CASELY-HAYFORD
SIMON ALLFORD
ANNA LAUB
JOHN MAYBURY
PHOEBE ENGLISH
ABIGAIL FLETCHER
NINA MAE FOWLER
PHILIP TSIARAS
PAUL SIMONON
CORTO MOLTEDO
DANIEL W. FLETCHER
EMMA WOOLLARD
DYLAN JONES
NOOMI RAPACE
ALEX MULLINS
CARLA GORDON
KIT KEMP

BEN HASSETT
ALEXANDRE DA CUNHA
JAIME PERLMAN
SOPHIE HERXHEIMER
FRANÇOISE DURAND
STEWART HELM
MARIO ROSSI
SIMONE GOOCH
JAIME GILI
BEN VAN BERKEL
PATCHARAVIPA BODIRATNANGKURA
PIERS ATKINSON
NIGEL COATES
MIHARA YASUHIRO
ROSEY CHAN
LIAM STEVENS
JESSE DARLING
RHONDA DRAKEFORD
DARCEL DISAPPOINTS
HATTIE STEWART
SOU FUJIMOTO
GREG WILLIAMS
RALPH STEADMAN
CLAIRE BARROW
VICTOR CRUZ
TANYA LING
GIRLI
ANNA PATERSON
SOFT BAROQUE
MISTY COPELAND & EVERETT DYSON
PAUL ANDREW
MARK LAZENBY
PREM SAHIB
BELLA FREUD
FRIENDSWITHYOU
ANDREW LOGAN
MIMI XU
YONATAN VINITSKY
SØLVE SUNDSBØ
MEREDITH OSTROM
DEENA ALJUHANI ABDULAZIZ
RACHEL ZOE
COLDEN DRYSTONE
SUZY MENKES
IDRIS KHAN
CHRIS MILTON
GARANCE DORÉ
MARCO DE VINCENZO
GEORGE BYRNE
SABINE GETTY
DSQUARED2
MARY KATRANTZOU
DELFINA DELETTREZ
WAYNE MASER
RHYS COREN
JOHN SQUIRE
PETRA NEMCOVA
MARCEL DZAMA
ORLA CAROLIN
JAY FIELDEN
OLYMPIA LE-TAN

BRUNA BISMARA
GEORGINA VON ETZDORF
STANLEY DONWOOD
VENETIA SCOTT
JAMES BALMFORTH
ROKSANDA ILINCIC
SUE WEBSTER
TIM NOBLE
DANNY CLINCH
PATRIK SCHUMACHER
HOLLY FULTON
MERLIN FERRY
ANDREW CULLOO
SCIASCIA GAMBACCINI
GIOJ DE MARCO
RICHARD YOUNG
ANTHONY WATSON
BARRY REIGATE
ARTHUR YATES
NINA CUCCHI
DARRELL VYDELINGUM
JENNY PACKHAM
HIKARI YOKOYAMA
NICOLAS SANTOS
ANNIE MORRIS
MAIA NORMAN
BILL MULLEN
EDDIE BORGO
JAMES MASSIAH
HUISHAN ZHANG
GIOVANNA BATTAGLIA ENGELBERT
ZOWIE BROACH
MELINA KAPPO-WEBBER
SARAH BURTON
SANDY RODRIGUEZ
ANGEL OTERO
ROBERT RABENSTEINER
HENRY STANFORD
ISABELLE STANISLAS
COCO GORDON MOORE
SHAUN MCDOWELL
JUERGEN TELLER
PATRICK KINMONTH
HANNA GARCIA FLEER
[FOR OFF WHITE C/O VIRGIL ABLOH™]
ALEX CHINNECK
GUILLAUME NERY
MOHAMMED QASIM ASHFAQ
LILY ASHLEY
RICHARD HAINES
EMILY JOHNSTON
ALLISON KATZ
BELLA HOWARD
CHARLIE WATTS
ANTON CORBIJN
JORDANA YECHIEL
AVAF
SHALA MONROQUE
JESSICA CHASTAIN
COLLEEN ATWOOD
AARON FAVALORO

JOHN BOOTH
ASHLEY WILLIAMS
KENGO KUMA
SCOTT STUDENBERG
FAYE TOOGOOD
CHRISTIAN MARCLAY
ALBER ELBAZ
JOHANNES HUEBL
RUPERT THOMAS
EMMA SUMMERTON
PIERRE D'AVOINE
CRAIG & KARL
SIMON CALLERY
EVA RICCOBONO
SHARON LEAHY-CLARK
AMBER ANDERSON
MARIA SOLE FERRAGAMO
CAROLINE ISSA
STEPHEN JONES
TONY CHAMBERS
RICCARDO POZZOLI
EVA CAVALLI DÜRINGER
OSANNA VISCONTI
SHEILA SRI PRAKASH
THOMAS PETHERICK
GAVIN TURK
PRINCESS JULIA
SUSAN HILLER
PETER SAVILLE
MASSIMO GIORGETTI
ANNE KOCH
BEN TURNBULL
ANGELA BIANI & MATILDA
SAMANTHA RAYE HOECHERL
LOTTE ANDERSEN
SIMON FUJIWARA
ALESSANDRO SARTORI
KIM CATTRALL
RICHARD LONG
LACHLAN BAILEY
HANS ULRICH OBRIST
MAX VADUKUL
SERGIO SARRI
JONATHAN YEO
DAVID ROWNTREE
JOHN BALDESSARI
FRANCESCO CARROZZINI
VALERIA NAPOLEONE
NEIL BARRETT
RAFAEL NADAL
LINDSAY ELLINGSON
TALI LENNOX
ANTONY GORMLEY
STEVE MCCURRY
MANDRAGORA
MARTYN BAL
MIKE FIGGIS
DAVID KOMA
JAMIE BOCHERT
SOFIA BARATTIERI
JJ MARTIN

SUSIE & NICK CAVE
BRANDON MAXWELL
PETITE MELLER
NINA YASHAR
MOSSET
JAMES CAPPER
TANCREDI DI CARCACI
POSY SIMMONDS
MARTA MARCÉ
FRANCA SOZZANI
KRIS RUHS
PAVITRA SRIPRAKASH
YVES SCHERER
DAVID KING REUBEN
DARIO CATELLANI
SHONA HEATH
JOANNA LUMLEY
GEORGINA GRAHAM
ANNA FRIEL
GIAMBATTISTA VALLI
MATTHEW BENJAMIN
RONNIE WOOD
ASHLEY HEATH

FIRST PUBLISHED IN ITALY
BY GRAFICHE OMNIA.